"*Branded Customer Service* packs the punches about really great customer service. It gives the reader an insight into how to differentiate through service and how to win. If you are really committed to getting the most out of your brand, read this book!"

—Mark Bergdahl, CEO, Customer Intimacy, Limited

"Any business that applies the on-brand ideas in this easy-to-read book will create a significant competitive advantage by converting its customers into apostles who will preach the gospel in the marketplace for that company."

—Dr. Tony Alessandra, author of *Collaborative Selling* and *The Platinum Rule*

"Barlow and Stewart have told the stories of some great customer service companies that have set the benchmark for their respective industries in building and delivering great brand promises. They get to the very essence of these customer service branding strategies by telling the how and why. A great read for anyone who is interested in customer service differentiation."

—Ralph Norris, Managing Director and CEO, Air New Zealand, Limited

"Barlow and Stewart reveal the secret of consumer loyalty. Consumers and companies alike should rejoice at the insights they offer."

—Rod Oram, business commentator

"I've always found effective branding to be as difficult to articulate as it is to do. For me it is a complex mix of creating an external perception that is also an internal reflection of who you are and what you stand for. *Branded Customer Service* is a great practical read for others who similarly wrestle with such concepts. It passed the get-real test for me and is certainly on-brand for what I want from TMI."

—Barbara Chapman, Head of Retail Banking and Marketing, ASB Bank

D0067407

"The future of branding is here now, and it requires a complete reassessment of your communication. This book opens your eyes to how simple it can be to assess and how powerful it can be to fix your branded customer service. This new level of brand building can become a long-term competitive advantage for your company."

—Jim Wagner, Senior Vice President, Mattel

"All too often we assume that branding is purely through the eyes of the customer. This book creates a refreshing perspective that our staff are the key to a successful brand. A straightforward and powerful interpretation using some great examples."

—Nigel Roberts, Managing Director, Langham Hotel, Hong Kong

"Extraordinary review and junction of branding approaches in the fields of products and services. This work can be done only by cooperation between practitioners on both sides of the table—branding products and branding services. Barlow and Stewart show how to brand services to match your brand promises."

—Uros Mocnik, General Manager, Business Knowledge, Croatia

"*Branded Customer Service* provides a road map to genuinely transform the customer experience that is accessible to all people within organizations—the concepts, language, and examples make sense whether you are a CEO or someone interacting with the customer moment by moment."

—Sonia Stojanovic, Head of Cultural Transformation, ANZ Banking Group

"What makes *Branded Customer Service* so powerful is that it's about action, not theory. Janelle Barlow and Paul Stewart get to the heart of how to make your business thrive by building a powerful brand and give you the steps to take that make it real. Buy this book now for every employee and take your company to the next level of competitive performance."

—Joe Calloway, author of *Becoming a Category of One*

"*Branded Customer Service* is a must-read for anyone in business committed to not only communicating what their brand is but practicing what their brand is. Barlow and Stewart unlock the processes for differentiating your business through branded customer service and then give you the key for attracting and retaining customers."

—David Lewis, Managing Director, VantagePoint Marketing Limited

"Brands create value if standards of performance are met every time the customer uses them. They cannot be dependent on the customer being fortunate enough to receive service from the best professional in the firm. Regardless of who serves the customer, a consistent quality of service must be provided and experienced for the brand to flourish. Janelle and Paul's groundbreaking research on this subject is essential for business success."

—Tom Grissen, CEO, Daon, former President and
General Manager, MAXIMUM

"Too many organizations are overpromising and underdelivering on their brand promises. Read this book for a foundation on which to base your customer service, for practical tips to shore up your service deficiencies, and for sustainable advantages you can shout about!"

—Bruce Scheer, Founder and Principal, FutureSight Consulting

"In a world where it's too easy to default to the tried and true, the generic, the same, this book makes a welcome stand for where brand needs to go. A wake-up call to companies worldwide—your customers are well and truly over vanilla."

—Mark Di Somma, Pusher, Audacity Group

"The strength of *Branded Customer Service* is in its clarity and pragmatism that sets out the map to think, feel, and act on a road to differentiate and to build much stronger brand equity. This book impresses me with more depth and significance on inside-out branding than any other I have previously experienced and stimulates thinking on what our organizations could become."

—David Walker, Executive Chairman, Walkers Advertising, Director, ICOM

"*Branded Customer Service* is not only well written, it shows in a very clear fashion how to incorporate brand into service delivery. This is easier said than done for all of us trying to build a service organization that takes advantage of strong brands. If you want practical advice that makes you think, this is the book for you."

—Sirish Mani, National Customer Service Center Operations Development Manager, Toyota Financial Services

"Just when I thought there was nothing left to say about branding and customer service, along come Janelle Barlow and Paul Stewart to prove me wrong. Filled with impeccable research, entertaining stories, masterful insight, and—most important—clear steps to follow, *Branded Customer Service* covers new and important ground. Read it, internalize it, and put it into practice—your customers will love you for it."

—Steve Farber, author of *The Radical Leap: A Personal Lesson in Extreme Leadership*

branded customer service

branded customer service
The New Competitive Edge

JANELLE BARLOW
and PAUL STEWART

BERRETT-KOEHLER PUBLISHERS, INC.
San Francisco

Berrett-Koehler Publishers, Inc.
235 Montgomery Street, Suite 650
San Francisco, CA 94104-2916
Tel: (415) 288-0260   Fax: (415) 362-2512   www.bkconnection.com

ORDERING INFORMATION

Quantity sales. Special discounts are available on quantity purchases by corporations, associations, and others. For details, contact the "Special Sales Department" at the Berrett-Koehler address above.

Individual sales. Berrett-Koehler publications are available through most bookstores. They can also be ordered direct from Berrett-Koehler: Tel: (800) 929-2929; Fax: (802) 864-7626; www.bkconnection.com

Orders for college textbook/course adoption use. Please contact Berrett-Koehler: Tel: (800) 929-2929; Fax: (802) 864-7626.

Orders by U.S. trade bookstores and wholesalers. Please contact Publishers Group West, 1700 Fourth Street, Berkeley, CA 94710. Tel: (510) 528-1444; Fax (510) 528-3444.

Berrett-Koehler and the BK logo are registered trademarks of Berrett-Koehler Publishers, Inc.

Printed in the United States of America

Berrett-Koehler books are printed on long-lasting acid-free paper. When it is available, we choose paper that has been manufactured by environmentally responsible processes. These may include using trees grown in sustainable forests, incorporating recycled paper, minimizing chlorine in bleaching, or recycling the energy produced at the paper mill.

Library of Congress Cataloging-in-Publication Data

Barlow, Janelle, 1943-
  Branded customer service : the new competitive edge / by
  Janelle Barlow and Paul Stewart.
    p. cm.
  Includes bibliographical references and index.
  ISBN 10: 1-57675-298-4; ISBN 13: 978-1-57675-298-2 (hardcover)
  ISBN 10: 1-57675-404-9; ISBN 13: 978-1-57675-404-7 (pbk.)
    1. Customer services. 2. Business names. 3. Brand name
  products. I. Stewart, Paul. II. Title.
HF5415.5.B3667 2004
658.8'12—dc22   2004047605

FIRST EDITION
10 09 08 07 06   10 9 8 7 6 5 4 3 2 1

Copyediting and proofreading by PeopleSpeak.
Book design by Designsmith Limited.
Composition by Beverly Butterfield, Girl of the West Productions.

This book is dedicated to long-suffering customers who have had the courage to remind companies that matching "what they do" with "what they promise" is not just a way to keep their business. It's a matter of common courtesy.

Contents

Foreword

A brand is not just a logo, an advertising slogan, a product, a service, a building, an airplane, great leadership, or profitability. A brand is all of these. It is the fabric of the organization woven together purposefully over a period of time. And it doesn't just happen, as Janelle Barlow and Paul Stewart so eloquently point out.

I had the opportunity to be the second CEO of Southwest Airlines when it was a fledgling company serving destinations in Texas. My role was to position the company with solid people, products, and a financial foundation for future growth with deregulation about to be enacted. One of my first priorities was to engage our senior management team in a visioning process. It was a small team of nine, including Chairman Herb Kelleher.

We went off-site to a conference room at a local university in Dallas, Texas, and I facilitated the session. The objective was to agree on a direction and pathway and distill down to a hundred words or less what we were going to be when we grew up. After ten hours of spirited discussion, we were all drained mentally and took the evening off for a cookout at my home. The following morning we started refreshed, and within an hour it became clear to all of us. *We were not an airline.*

We were in mass transportation, a totally different business, a different model, a different brand. We could create new fliers and markets with low costs, low fares, frequent service, and great people, competing with the automobile, the bus, and the living room—not other airlines.

We then wrote a mission/vision statement that was only fifty-two words long and easily understood by all our stakeholders. Taking the next step—developing a culture to support the brand—required spending a lot of time the following year spreading that gospel, one-on-one, one-on-two, wherever we could find an audience.

You don't take a commodity, an airline seat, and turn it into a recognizable brand unless all of your teammates buy into and benefit from the proposition. Southwest has always believed in "hiring attitudes and teaching skills" and sharing the profits with all employees. We believed that if we treated our people as number one, they would treat our customers the same way. As two advertising executives from New York, Simon and Gromes, once said to me: "If you just sell a product or a service you will probably be known as a vendor or supplier. If you sell a vision or experience you will begin to develop a brand."

It has worked successfully as Southwest has been profitable every year for nearly thirty years, a record unmatched in a turbulent industry. If you are serious about building great enduring connections between your customers and the brand you represent, then *Branded Customer Service* will provide you both the road map and the toolkit you need to become an on-brand organization and create the success Southwest Airlines, a brand pioneering company, has enjoyed.

Howard Putnam
Former CEO of Southwest Airlines

Acknowledgments

Thank you for helping keep us on-brand!

Any strong brand is an orchestration of dozens, even hundreds, of component parts. The same is true of any book. They are never written in isolation, so thanks go everywhere, but responsibility lies with the authors.

We particularly want to thank clients and customers who engaged us in conversation on this topic and helped us think through the tricky conceptual parts of this book. And thanks to service providers, even when they gave us off-brand service, so we could experience at a strong emotional level what happens when a brand promise is authentically delivered—or not.

To all the named, and unnamed, researchers who have toiled over these concepts, crunched the numbers, and bothered to write it all down in business journals, we give you a resounding *thank you!* This work is not easy, and we are mindful of how the carefully measured thinking of academicians inspired our thinking on the subject.

To the many people who reviewed the text, especially in its early formative stages, we thank you for seeing the genesis of an idea that has the potential to impact customer service for a long time. And to the dozens of people who read the book before it was in its final form and still wrote glowing testimonials, we are totally indebted. To such inspired people as Felicity Stevens, David Walker, Mark Di Somma, and Grant Costello, with whom we have been privileged to work on brand projects over the years, we are indebted to you for shaping our initial understanding around brand strategy and internal branding.

Berrett-Koehler has again lived up to its brand promise in how its staff worked with us. Steven Piersanti, publisher, truly stayed on-brand in his no-holds-barred feedback, necessitating us to write and rewrite. We especially appreciate his approaching us about this book. Once Janelle suggested the idea for the book, Steven held on to the vision throughout two years of telephone calls. Our gratitude also goes to Kerenza Smith, who at the eleventh hour helped us to resolve issues we had been grappling with in relation to the creative design, Beverly Butterfield for final composition, and Sharon Goldinger for her excellent copyediting.

Our TMI colleagues, staff, and friends around the world have been exceptionally generous with their time and feedback. They include Jeffrey Mishlove, Lewis Barlow, Pamela Fedderson, Leah Fisher, Jennifer Schmicher, Bill Oden, Peta Peter, Ralph Simpfendorfer, Judith and Dick Davidson, Elcee Villa, Debbie Schultz, Vic Hewson, George Aveling, and a host of our colleagues. Thank you for your interest and thank you for living the brand TMI. And a special thanks to Howard Putnam, not just for his writing the foreword to this book, but also for participating in the vision of Southwest Airlines to show that branded customer service can be done!

Finally, we want to thank the many organizations and individuals who have asked us to work with them on this topic, either by consulting with them on their service branding needs or by inviting us to deliver keynote speeches on the topic. Every good speaker knows that there is no better way to grasp a topic than being asked to speak about it.

Introduction

On-Brand or Off-Brand

What is a brand?

At its most basic level, a brand is a unique identity. It is a shorthand way the public thinks about what you do, produce, serve, and sell.

When well conceived and developed, a brand is a vibrant picture held in consumers' minds. Well-executed brands are worth millions, even billions of dollars, in sales and shareholder value. Brands stand out like beacons of light in a sea awash with high-quality products and services offered to meet consumer-expression needs, as consumers choose brands in great part to tell the world and themselves who they are. Branding is a central element of marketing strategies. The consumer in effect believes, "The only way I can be who I am is to have specific products or services." A powerful brand, therefore, creates a must-have quasi monopoly for itself.

So, what is branded customer service?

It's an additional and huge way to further distinguish a brand's unique identity. Branded customer service goes way beyond generic service. It even is more than excellent service. It is a strategic and organized way to deliver on-brand customer experiences that magnify brand promises. It adds value to target markets by driving home the essence of a brand. In so doing, branded customer service can become so valuable that it takes on the power of a brand unto itself.

When service experiences are aligned with brand promises, a multiplying effect occurs that is significantly more engaging than just a well-recognized brand name. When service experiences do not match brand promises, as so frequently happens, trust is undermined and brand erosion occurs. This gap is costly and can ruin or seriously diminish a good advertising campaign. For all these reasons, branded customer service is the new competitive edge in the service economy.

Some time ago, an Australian bank made a promise that customers would be given $5 if they had to wait longer than five minutes for a teller. The promise (with its well-crafted subtext message that the bank valued its customers' time so much that they would never waste more than five minutes of it) attracted customers. Unfortunately, the bank failed in its delivery. Employees got so hassled trying to deliver on the unrealistic, maximum-five-minute promise that the bank had to retract its promise. The result? Immediate, widely publicized, and significant brand erosion.

On the other hand, another bank has successfully integrated its brand advertising into its service culture. The bank recently measured the impact of its advertising, comparing reactions of customers with noncustomers. The research concluded that customers *who had both seen the bank's advertisements and experienced its service* had the strongest positive associations with the brand's attributes, which are listed on the following chart.

Customers who had merely experienced the bank's service without seeing the ads had a lower association with the bank's brand attributes. And for noncustomers who saw the ads but did not receive any rein-forcement through service of the brand promise, the associations with the attributes were still lower. Conclusion: *a combination of strong advertising* to let customers know what they should expect *and then consistently delivering* the advertised service results in the most positive brand associations, as figure 1 illustrates.[1]

Figure 1. The power of branded service experiences In reinforcing advertising

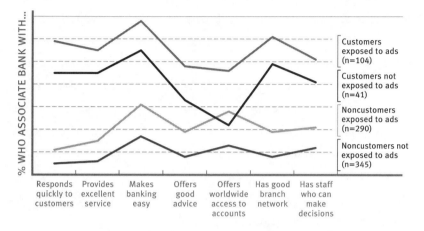

This research, based on 780 interviews conducted between January and March 2002, demonstrates that there is a real market opportunity for companies to forge stronger relationships with customers. Such relationships take advantage of the multiplying effect of actually delivering *unique* service experiences that have been promised in advertising, via public relations, or on the Web. When service is branded and combined with a solid product offering, you have a winning combination that can reduce the impact of your competitors. It will be difficult, in fact, for others to copy you if you continually reinforce and magnify your unique brand position through parallel service delivery.

Brand promises meet customers' psychological needs beyond the simple and functional. Even though brands speak to large population groups, customers experience them as personal connections to products and services. This personal connection is what creates brand engagement and commitment. As actor and film producer Robert Redford says, "If it's not personal, then there won't be any passion or commitment."[2]

We predict that in a few years, businesses will make a clear distinction between generic customer service and branded customer service. The distinction between old-fashioned, good generic service and branded customer service will be understood in the same way that the marketplace today understands the distinction between generic products and branded products—such as with generic prescription drugs versus brand-name drugs. We further predict that *on-brand service,* a term we use to describe customer service that is aligned with brand promises, will become the standard that twenty-first-century businesses use to judge service. Once people are introduced to the terms *on-brand* and *off-brand,* they immediately grasp the concept and understand how on- and off-brand service is not identical to good and bad service.

This book outlines ways to reinforce both the logical and emotional aspects of your brand through service delivery. We consider *brands when they are seen through the focus of customer service.* We also reverse the proposition and consider *customer service when it is seen through the focus of branding.* Whichever way you look at it, our ultimate goal is to help you build equity for your brand (increased name recognition, more loyal customers, increased market share, and higher margins) by offering you a standard by which to craft the human part of your customer service so it stays on-brand. You can then take advantage of what branding experts have long known: a strong brand is indeed a very valuable asset.

Finally, as customers raise the bar on the service they expect, organizations that do not brand their service offerings will be at a distinct disadvantage. We will show you how to align the dynamics of your customer service in Redford's "passionate and committed" way with the promises and *persona* of your carefully defined brand. This book will show you what is necessary to avoid being left behind.

Why this book now?

Despite all the money invested in branding, most brands underperform. The major reason for this is that most branding strategies today still rely heavily on advertisements, marketing, endorsements, and other media-based approaches in an economy that has become predominantly service based. We contend that organizations can gain the maximum return from brand expenditures when everyone—rather than just the marketing department—reinforces the brand.

Service organizations continue to use, without much questioning, branding models that are more appropriate to fast-moving consumer goods, or FMCG. The key element in the chain, the actual service experience, is often overlooked because either advertising agencies and traditional marketers typically do not have core competencies in this area or they do not have the mandate to shape and influence it. The service component of the brand experience is therefore a powerful competitive weapon, waiting to be unleashed. As one hotelier recently remarked to us, "Our marketing collateral is very good. But do we deliver? If we really delivered what we imply, our customer-return rate would be much higher."

For this reason, this book focuses on the two main organizational audiences that need more than image-based strategies to gain maximum market share: those that are exclusively service based and those that are product based but with a large component of service. When a large part of what you have to offer consumers is delivered through people, customer experiences that reinforce your brand messages are perhaps the most enduring means of keeping and even getting customers. James Gilmore and Joe Pine, authors of *The Experience Economy*, express a viewpoint that has become widely accepted: "People have become relatively immune to messages targeted at them. The way to reach your customers is to create an experience within them."[3]

We were inspired to write *Branded Customer Service* after surveying the market and exchanging ideas with a number of our consulting clients and other experts in the field of branding. We came to the conclusion that if advertising dollars and marketing efforts communicate one brand message and staff deliver something different, an organization is wasting money and probably has an image problem!

We read countless pages of literature on branding and discovered a marketplace filled with books and articles written predominantly by branding experts—not customer service experts. Many recently released books do discuss the importance of customer service in brand development, but they are extremely broad in their coverage and primarily address how organizational culture supports delivery of the brand. While addressing important topics, these books give little mention to what we see is one of the most important and yet overlooked topics in this field: how employees can actually deliver their organizational brands when they are engaged in activity that directly or indirectly affects customers.

It is very useful for a retail chain of stores, for example, that makes a brand promise to "always be there to help customers" to align its material service (processes, product availability and range, opening hours, and locations) to deliver that promise. However, the brand promise will still fall short if the store employees do not understand the importance of their own behavior in supporting this brand promise.

For example, if employees stand in rapt conversation with each other—in full view of a long line of customers waiting to be served—that will be experienced as off-brand by customers. Staff may miss the point that their "innocent" behavior, however justified it may be, erodes confidence in the retail chain's brand position as much as an ineffective advertisement can turn off customers. A brand statement can be made with off-brand nonverbal staff behavior: "We say we are, but, in fact, we aren't always there to help you." The brand effort is hijacked—or at best, is not taken advantage of—unless employees are aware of and understand the consequences of *all* their brand-related behaviors.

What flocking birds can teach us about branded service

As customer service consultants, we know it is possible, though not easy, to align personal service behaviors with brand promises in a memorable way that is not scripted. A metaphor we find inspiring is the rapid, darting, swirling patterns that large flocks of flying birds produce without colliding into each other. The red-billed quelea, the most common wild bird on this planet, is known to swarm in flocks a million strong and at the same time display eye-popping swirling patterns. While the physics that explains this remarkable phenomenon is complex, basically the birds follow three simple self-organizing principles that enable this complex group activity—even though each single bird's pattern is individual. Using their keen eyesight and rapid turning ability, the birds follow three simple rules: (1) avoid bumping into each other, (2) fly at the same speed, and (3) head towards the center of their group.[4]

We believe the way flocking birds do this can bring understanding to how service can both be branded and yet also utilize the potentiality that unique human-to-human contact enjoys. While marketers can fairly easily present one consistent external face of the brand, delivering consistent customer service that enhances the brand is another matter altogether. Customer service is offered by humans, who are highly individualistic. As a result, the temptation is strong to script service in order to control its variation. We argue that this is not a good idea—even to honor the brand.

The historical bias toward the tightly managed approach for fast-moving consumer goods no doubt explains why the same tight controls are frequently applied to customer service exchanges. Most marketing professionals cut their teeth managing FMCG using rigid mandates that work well with products that are relatively inexpensive and purchased in high quantities. All too often, they extend this practice by scripting what service providers say to customers and by defining precise service behaviors. Many marketing professionals really believe that if you print "thank you" on a sales slip it deftly handles the issue of gratitude for a customer's business. Unfortunately, this rule-driven scripting can lead to inauthentic exchanges that leave customers either feeling ambivalent or scratching their heads in wonderment about the service they have received. It can also lead to bored, underutilized, and frustrated staff.

We believe that it is possible to use brand promises, which are generally presented in easy-to-understand and uncluttered concepts, as the self-organizing "flocking" guidelines to focus on-brand customer service delivered by thousands of employees in large organizations. In this way, branded customer service can be presented in a patterned way, an on-brand way that still takes advantage of individual input.

It is possible, in fact, to get so good at delivering branded customer service that your staff-customer interactions can cover a multitude of material deficits in your product offering. Even when this happens, brand-congruent service interactions enable customers to walk away with crystal clarity and trust that they received the promises of your advertising and marketing efforts. However, simply delivering good service, or as we refer to it, generic customer service, no longer is enough to distinguish a business's products and services.

Advertising agencies focus carefully on all the nuances of ads they create for clients and their brands. They pay attention to precise color hues, every single word, voice tonality, music, images, spokespeople.

They do this to enhance and manage unique images. The cover of this book, as a case in point, was designed by a brand image consultant. While someone who picks up this book may not understand all the dynamics that have been elegantly designed into the words, word placement, typesetting, and colors, the designer had a clear sense of creating a cover that enhances the content of this book. Branded customer service is also about subtlety of emphasis, the subtlety of staff behavior that reinforces an image and brand in every way possible.

Mercedes-Benz, for example, is concerned with luxury and solid engineering and focuses heavily on the passenger's experience. BMW, by contrast, is focused on performance and the driver's experience. Because each company delivers on its product promises and large population niches like what each offers, both brands command price premiums. When you walk into a BMW dealership, you will more than likely be treated to a service experience that is also about performance. Someone will normally be at your side in thirty seconds, focused, and fast in both behavior and speech. Chris Howe, with the UK company ChangeMaker, labels the BMW process as "engineered."[5] He describes the Mercedes experience as more relaxed, smoother, unobtrusive, and professional, in a way so you know you have "just spoken to Mercedes-Benz." BMW and Mercedes staff have to understand branding messages very well to be able to deliver consistent experiences like this.

Many times customers are not able to describe exactly what happens in branded service exchanges. For example, most people cannot articulate the difference between a BMW and a Mercedes sales pitch. But customers walk away from these dealerships with their perceptions of these auto brands intensified in the same way as actually test-driving a BMW or Mercedes reinforces brand promises. Using the simple, elegantly designed, organizing principles that describe their brands, BMW and Mercedes are both good at inspiring their sales teams and service departments to deliver their brand pledges.

As generic copies of brand-name products are slowly chipping away at the name-recognition advantage that well-known brands enjoy, many companies have learned that the impact of advertising and marketing alone is not enough to push revenue growth. Because generic brands can cleverly cash in on a branded product's cachet by imitating packaging and lowering prices, brands today have to be bigger than the label, bigger than the box, bigger than the product.

Branded Customer Service provides hands-on, tested processes and ideas that can be adapted to make unique brands bigger. Some of these are simple and easy to implement. Others require extensive integration of brand values within your organizational culture.

A number of companies have branded their service. Some of them are mentioned in this book. Others are making the attempt. But most are mired in their efforts to offer good, generic customer service that is frankly insufficiently related to the brand they represent. Most brand and marketing experts do not understand how to brand service. On the other hand, while most customer service experts are able to delineate components of good customer service, they rarely take this concept a step further to focus on brand-specific customer service. They are, therefore, neglecting a key part of business strategy. This book was written to bridge this large gap and make a unique contribution to the fields of branding and customer service.

How to use this book

This book walks you through a wide array of ideas, research, strategies, and techniques to facilitate your understanding and delivery of your brand through service. It is divided into three parts:

- Part I: Linking the Big World of Branding to Customer Service
- Part II: Embedding On-Brand Service into Your Organizational DNA
- Part III: The Branded Customer Service Toolbox

While each of the three parts of this book can stand alone, we encourage you to at least skim the contents even if you find yourself concentrating on one part more than another. We have organized the material in a way that makes logical sense to us. However, your own expertise may inspire you to explore it in a different order.

Part I: Linking the Big World of Branding to Customer Service covers the evolution and power of brands and argues that generic customer service does not take advantage of the uniqueness of each brand's values and promises. We contend that generic customer service is minimally competitive in today's service economy and look at what is necessary for you to develop a strategy that integrates your brand into the heart of your customer service delivery. This part of the book links branding concepts to the idea of branded customer service. Challenges to branding your customer service are highlighted, and a road map is presented to start you on your way. Examples of on-brand service and off-brand service are sprinkled throughout this section.

Most research journals are filled with articles that are detailed, complex, and often incomprehensible to anyone who is not a marketing or brand expert or someone not well versed in statistical methods. Therefore, we have summarized branding literature to make it more accessible to those primarily interested in customer service or management. For those who are well versed in the literature, we have linked branding with customer service concepts to provide a new view for brand experts.

Part II: Embedding On-Brand Service into Your Organizational DNA explores ways to support and promote your branded customer service through initiatives involving culture change, leadership communication, the manager's role, and brand champions. In this part, we also place special emphasis on the importance of human resources (HR) strategies and functions in ensuring brand alignment. We endorse the groundswell to house the function of brand building in both marketing and HR departments. In fact, we firmly believe that HR has the potential to play a make-or-break role in successful branded service initiatives. Managers, human resource professionals, and trainers will find this section of the book particularly valuable.

We begin the second part of this book with a full explanation of the model that TMI, our training and consulting company, uses. The chapter called "Defining Your Brand DNA" describes our philosophy and explains how we work at staying on-brand ourselves.

Part III: The Branded Customer Service Toolbox is designed as a toolbox of methodologies and practical ideas that will guide you in delivering service that is aligned to your brand. Just as branding techniques need to be adapted for each product or service, there is no one best way to brand your customer service. We offer many exercises in part III, which are all most effective when adapted to your unique brand offering. The dozens of exercises and ideas we share, tested for more than two decades, are representative of the types we use with our own clients and should be seen as prototypes. We always adapt these ideas to the unique brand promises of the organizations with which we work, and you must do the same for your own organization. Think of these exercises as engines that gain power as they are customized to your specific brand.

We also cover the imperative of sales, service, and brand linkage in part III. We look at what happens when salespeople focus on delivering their brand to customers instead of focusing on whether they have met their quotas. Service staff also better deliver the brand to customers when they understand that they, too, directly influence sales.

If you read part III first to get to the Toolbox section, we encourage you to then read parts I and II. The context for these exercises is provided in parts I and II, and context is important to fully understand and implement them.

Who this book is for

This book is written for those who want to unleash the full potential of their brands and make their customer service so distinct that it has as much value as their brand idea possesses. It is also for those who understand that making customer service central to brand identity is not a one-time or simple task but a strategic decision. It entails a transformational process for your entire organization. We are enamored with Jim Collins's statement in *Good to Great,* in which he describes companies that undergo transformation as having "no single defining action, no grand program, no one killer innovation, no solitary lucky break, no miracle moment. Rather the process resemble[s] relentlessly pushing a giant heavy flywheel in one direction, turn upon turn, building momentum until a point of breakthrough, and beyond."[6]

Brand experts Bob Tyrell and Tim Westall make the same point with a slightly different caution. "Branding customer service requires something much more complex than the bolt-on activities currently parading as 'relationship' building. It implies developing a recognizable style and personality, and that has important implications for brand marketing."[7]

Because of this complexity, we address four audiences, each with a different role to play when service experiences are branded.

1. *Executives in top-level positions.* Executives who read this book will gain an overview of how the focus of branded customer service can help integrate *all* the elements of their business. Once made, this decision is not one to be taken lightly and changed every time there is a shift in leadership. Executives also need to recognize the impact they themselves have as representatives and champions of the brand to both customers and employees.

2. *Those with responsibility for shaping the environment in which on-brand service is delivered.* This second audience includes marketing specialists, human resource professionals, and customer service trainers. All three groups need to understand what is possible with branded service, what is required to make it happen, and how they must cooperate in this venture.

3. *Those who supervise and manage others who have direct contact with customers.* Branding is such an essential topic in today's business world that everyone who represents your business needs a deeper understanding of the phenomenon.

4. *Those who have direct contact with customers.* All service delivery will benefit from a deeper understand of branding.

Whether you are a service provider—and most of us have some aspect of service provision in our work—a manager of service providers, or a builder of brands, *Branded Customer Service* offers you a context to think about your own behavior in relationship to your organization's brand promises. It will guide you through the demanding task of lining up behaviors until you know in your bones that you are doing more than just meeting a payroll—or earning a paycheck.

We know from experience that it is possible to educate large percentages of the workforce to deliver a service style that is uniquely defined for the organization they represent. At the same time, we do not believe that this happens by accident or as a flight of fancy. And once achieved, the work to keep your brand alive within your organization is ongoing and just as demanding and critical as the effort to get it there in the first place.

Part I

Linking the Big World of Branding to Customer Service

Because of the huge sums of money invested in brands and the billions of dollars of shareholder value they represent, marketing professionals know a great deal about the subject. They know how branding works, its components, and what it takes to create a brand leader.

Brand fads appear from time to time, not so dissimilar from Andy Warhol's fifteen-minutes-of-fame concept. Yet there is a sufficient mystery that leaves even the most rigorous marketers in awe of successful brands, especially the immediately recognized ones that have maintained their appeal over long periods of time.

This section of the book establishes a backdrop against which you can evaluate how to brand your service experiences. You will be introduced to language that cuts to the quick in determining if your service is on-brand or off-brand. You will also become acquainted with organizations that have done well with their service branding—and those that have not.

At the end of part I, you should be able to decide whether you want to take the next steps in linking your service delivery to your brand and what those next steps should be.

1

The Branding Imperative

Branding is one of the hottest topics in business today. It has become the business buzzword. Indeed, some refer to it as a Branding Revolution.[1] The reason couldn't be more straightforward and underscores a clear business message in today's crowded marketplace: your brand defines the unique point of differentiation for your products and services and is, perhaps, your only real opportunity to stand out.

Branding: a way of doing business

The paramount role that brands and branding now play has been accompanied by major shifts in the field of marketing. Brands are seen to be much more than names or logos. Brands are as much a way of doing business as they are a reputation or identity.

The London-based branding agency Brand Guardians describes the linkage this way: "Branding is about performance. Branding represents different things to different people. But in the final analysis, branding is a tool for delivering your business objectives: a means to an end, not an end in itself."[2]

Judgments about brands are structured with logical evaluation and laced with emotion. Some brand experts believe that a brand is *predominantly* an emotional judgment. UK marketing agency Ogilvy-One's research, for example, suggests that as much as 66 percent of the preference for a brand is driven by emotional elements—even if consumers believe they are making rational decisions.[3]

Because brands are largely *perceptions,* even though organizations today increasingly count brand strength as a key corporate asset, it makes sense to argue that brands are not exclusively owned by organizations. They are co-owned by consumers and organizations, equity partners in their shared relationship. This perceived co-ownership leads consumers to believe they are "owed" delivery of what they have been promised.

off-brand

Janelle walked into a Rite Aid store. Over the entrance was a big, riveting sign that read "The Customer Is # 1." After picking up some items, Janelle went to stand in the only open check stand line, a queue that had three people in it. The customer whose items were being rung up was surprised at the price of one of them. She said, "Oh, I didn't realize it was that price. I don't think I want it if it's that much." The clerk sighed and picked up the intercom telephone to page the manager. "I need some help with the cash register. Could the manager please come to the front of the store?"

Everyone waited while the line grew in length. The manager did not arrive. The clerk once again got on the paging system to announce to the entire store, "Would the manager please come to the front of the store. I need to reverse an item out!" Again, nothing. In the meantime, the customer was beginning to show signs of embarrassment as the line continued to grow. She knew she was holding all of us up.

Still nothing happened. The line now had eight people in it. The clerk, in exasperation, then shouted, not even bothering to use the intercom, "I need the manager right away. The customer thinks this item is too expensive."

The manager slowly sauntered to the front of the store, ignoring the long line of customers and the very embarrassed woman. The manager reached inside her smock and pulled out a key that she stuck into the cash register to release a lock. Now the clerk could reverse out the item. Without a word to anyone, the manager then proceeded to return to the back of the store.

As Janelle walked out the store, she once again noted the banner, "The Customer Is # 1." Right!

Companies promote their services and products by elevating consumer expectations and then act surprised when customers report that they feel like they got a bucket of cold water tossed in their faces. We believe it is reasonable and even predictable that consumers will feel this way because delivery of promises is frequently so different from how they are sold or how they look in ads or on Web sites. On the other hand, a simple and friendly hello using a customer's name and a quick response to an e-mail can send a nonverbal message that reinforces a larger more complicated promise: "We are big enough to meet your immediate business needs while we are small enough to know you."

Brand researchers have come to a profound conclusion with far-ranging impact: marketing must involve more than advertising and public relations. Branding success is no longer predominantly measured by how many consumers recognize or are aware of brands and their logos or slogans but by how strongly consumers feel connected to brands.

In fact, if advertising recognition is the sole criterion for marketing success, ad agencies are not doing a very good job. A recent survey by the brand consulting company Emergence found that of twenty-two taglines (McDonald's "You deserve a break today" is an example of a tagline) of the companies spending the most on advertising in the United States, only six were recognized by more than 10 percent of those surveyed.[4] Even when recognized, many advertising slogans are stated in absolute terms, such as The Customer Is # 1 or The Customer Is Always Right or 100% Satisfaction Guaranteed. The head of Emergence, Kelly O'Keefe, suggests that such statements don't work because a large proportion of the public believes they are mostly hype.[5]

Brands: a compelling point of differentiation

Branding occurs when a distinct head and heart response happens in relationship to a company symbol or logo. This reaction is the purpose of branding because positive thoughts and feelings inspire behaviors such as speaking favorably about services and products, joining clubs that relate to brands, paying higher prices, tolerating errors and shortfalls, and purchasing more of branded products and services. Today's brands are likely to be seen as living entities complete with personalities. Elaborate stories are built around them that companies hope are elicited with a minimum of stimulation every time a consumer has contact with their brands.

The first step in branding is to create a compelling, consistent, and sustainable point of differentiation. Differentiation, in the words of brand experts Young and Rubican, "is about making the brand greater than its individual parts."[6] Your competitors by and large possess your "individual parts." The task of branding is to figure out how your *combined offerings* create a value proposition that is unique.

Without this differentiation, products, services, and entire organizations enter what some refer to as the "gray zone,"[7] where customers are unable to distinguish what you do from what everybody else does. They cannot describe your offerings in a few simple words. Neither do they feel connected to your brand, edging you perilously close to becoming a commodity. Unfortunately, this happens all too often. As Patrick Gourney, former CEO of the Body Shop, points out, "Lack of differentiation is not something you notice straight away as a brand owner, but it creeps up on you and then it's too late."[8]

Historically, companies have used differentiation to influence consumer perceptions, expectations, and purchasing decisions primarily through the power of advertising and public relations. After all, when executed effectively, marketing attracts the right customers from a targeted market segment and delivers them to the organization. The organization must then begin to take advantage of these marketing successes. One of the best ways to engage customers in long-term relationships is to consistently deliver, both logically and emotionally, the brand promise. When this happens, brands are noticeably intensified. An alignment will occur between the assurance about "who you are and what you stand for" and the reality of "what you do and what you deliver."

Your brand in action

No doubt, traditional value aspects of branding have changed and will continue to do so. The old image appeal of brands, for example, no longer attracts in quite the same way as it once did. But there is no conclusive evidence that branding has lost pull—when it is done well. In fact, based on her research, Harvard professor Susan Fournier contends brands continue to "serve as powerful repositories of meaning . . . employed in the substantiation, creation, and production of concepts of self in the marketing age."[9]

Consumers "own" their brands: the case of Starship

When brand meanings have been established and are alive in the hearts and minds of customers, they feel possessive toward "their" brands. This becomes very evident when companies try to tamper with them. A poignant example happened when the Auckland, New Zealand, District Health Board decided in early 2003 to do away with Starship, a much-loved hospital. Starship is a specialist children's hospital that has built a stellar reputation of strength and compassion for treating children with life-threatening illnesses. It offers its young patients, and their families and friends, a unique experience that alleviates the fear and sadness associated with most intensive medical care. Its taglines are "Giving children the best possible chance" and "Family centered care in a child focused environment."[10]

When given the much broader responsibility of delivering the best possible health services across the full spectrum of health care, the Auckland Health Board had a new modern facility built to house both Starship and a number of different specialist hospitals. Part of this standardization process involved changing the names of the hospitals, including Starship. After it became known that Starship would become the bland-sounding Auckland City Hospital Children's Services, the nationwide reaction was swift, unanticipated, and vociferous. A highly charged public debate erupted with stakeholders of all types (former patients, parents, staff, and the general public) rejecting the name change and criticizing the health board.

Nothing articulated the issue better, nor provided a more compelling explanation of what brands are about, than this letter published in a New Zealand national newspaper.

Our family has been traveling frequently to Auckland for two years, for cancer treatment for our eight year old daughter. The emotional value to us, knowing Holly is being treated and cared for at Starship, is huge. The word encompasses times of hope, fear, worry and sadness for ourselves as well as other children and families we have met there.

So, yes our attachment to the name is emotive . . . But what makes it a world-class facility is the emotive stuff which the staff excel in— the things we have trouble putting a value on—such as compassion, patience, love and commitment. Mr. Brown [Auckland Health Board] is quoted as saying there is nothing special about the children's hospital . . . this narrow view is not appropriate for the chairman of a district health board as it signifies he is not in touch with the nature and the purpose of this facility.[11]

Brands are names, logos, beliefs—and experiences

Any brand is clearly more than just its name. Brands are the values, beliefs, and service experiences that underpin them as the Starship case so poignantly expresses. When put this way, it is easy to see how customer service is a brand in action. A belief that Starship's staff would continue to deliver to a specific set of values was solidified in people who had personally experienced the hospital. In Starship's case, the customers obviously feared that with a name change, the experiences associated with the brand would be lost as well.

The history of branding as it relates to the customer experience

Somebody once said that the history of branding could be summed up in three simple phrases: This is mine. I am better. I am like this. In other words, brands as ownership, brands as snob appeal, and brands as self-expression.[12]

The genesis of the word *brand* is Middle English, and it means a flame or torch. Philip Ross, with Business Specialties, comes closest to a definition of branding that we endorse: "Branding as we know it today is the art of instilling and communicating the values and character of a company or organization through association with its logo. Psychology calls it symbolic association and finds it to be foundational to the learning process."[13] This definition is not too far astray from the rather perky notion by research consultants Wendy Gordon and Sally Ford-Hutchinson, who write, "A brand is a metaphor for a complex pattern of associations that exists in the heads of individuals (customers/consumers/users), not in the heads of the marketing department."[14]

The practice of branding has been around for a long time. A trademark can be found on the bottom of a sandal dated from 200 BC.[15] For two thousand years, Christian brands have included the fish and cross. Brands were once used to mark and punish criminals. Ranchers scored brands on the hides of cattle to establish ownership, especially useful at a time when the majority of the population could not read.

Modern brands include Smirnoff, which originated in the twelfth century. In the 1870s George Eastman began the brand Kodak, with its well-known commitment to making photographic memories. General Electric, a consistently strong brand, was created in 1896.

The father of advertising, Earnest Elmo Calkins (1868–1964), was the first to suggest that products actually encompassed people's ideals.[16] Products, Calkins argued, reflected the aspirations that people held about themselves, their families, and their positions in society.

Brands and their links to psychological and social benefits

Because of the wealth that many middle-class people had begun to accumulate, Calkins believed they were less interested in the functional benefits of products. Due in large part to Calkins's influence, advertising began to focus on the psychological and social benefits that came from using and acquiring products. Advertisers linked product and service attributes to values that people considered important in their lives. This inspired media expert Marshall McLuhan to say, "Historians and archaeologists will one day discover that the ads of our time are the richest and most faithful daily reflections any society ever made of its whole range of activities."[17]

By the late 1920s, economists were paying close attention to the economic potential of branding, primarily influenced by Procter & Gamble's brand management system. P&G advertised Oxydol detergent in its sponsorship of daytime radio serials. Forty million people tuned in, and P&G benefited from a dramatic leap in sales that became a gold mine for it. Other soap companies followed P&G's practice, and hence today we have "soap operas."

J. Robinson, a noted economist of the 1930s, emphasized the inherent economic value of widely recognized trademarks: "Various brands of a certain article which in fact are almost exactly alike may be sold at different qualities under names and labels which will induce rich and snobbish buyers to divide themselves from the poor buyers."[18]

Branding helps focus attention

Today we understand that the concept of branding is a lot more than snob appeal, as Robinson implies. In the last eighty years, branding has moved to the innermost core of business marketing functions. Today many people, such as musicians, actors, entertainers, and even some businesspeople, view themselves as brands when just a few years ago they would have felt cheapened to think of themselves this way.

When used to describe people or cities, branding helps focus attention on a few characteristics. Las Vegas is commonly described in branding terms ("What happens here, stays here," "The World's Most Entertaining City," "The Capital of Family Entertainment," and even "Sin City"), and other cities are beginning to follow suit. Branding as a concept has changed forever the way people in businesses and organizations think about themselves. As social commentator Laura Barton notes, "Our expectations of how life should be are bigger, brighter, bolder than reality could ever hope to be."[19]

Yet we are just scratching the surface potential of the brand concept. Branding continues to evolve at the same pace as the market economy evolves. The idea of branding is also being shaped by brand experts themselves, two of which wistfully remarked, "In branding much is said, much is claimed, much is being done, but there remains much to be known."[20]

Branding as an evolving concept

Because the field is so rapidly changing, once we think we fully comprehend consumers' relationships to brands, we should also be willing to broaden, deepen, or switch our thinking. For example, consider the question, Why do people choose one brand over another when the products are almost identical? Marketers will tell you that consumers do not choose Coca-Cola over Pepsi, or vice versa, because of the ingredients of the two soft drinks. Rather, consumers unconsciously decide which *brand message,* Coca-Cola's or Pepsi's, suits them better—even though consumers insist they make their decisions on taste.

At face value, that sounds simple enough. But how does this happen? Rory Morgan, group marketing sciences director at the London-based WPP Group, dissects three emotional factors—authority, identification, and social approval—that account for that simple choice of Coke or Pepsi.[21]

While Morgan's model is beyond the scope of this book, he exemplifies just one of many who use sophisticated statistical techniques to provide a more complete understanding of the psychological dimensions and drivers of brands. We must take these models into account, however, or run the risk of not fully comprehending the power of branding and missing the opportunities it offers.

Brands hold their own attitudes

Some brand experts even suggest that what brands "think" about consumers should be considered. For example, what does Rolex, the luxury watch, think about you? This is an interesting question, and one answer—"You're not good enough for a Rolex"—stops many people from even considering its purchase. The reasoning is that if there is a genuine relationship between customers and brands, then they both must have opinions of each other—even though the consumer holds both opinions.[22]

Consider a small company wanting to use the services of a large consulting firm. The owners of the small company may never even call to find out whether that is a viable idea if they perceive the consulting firm only wants to deal with large Fortune 100 companies. This may not be the case. The consulting firm may actually welcome the business of a small company. But in order to demonstrate its competency, the consulting firm will list its largest, most well-known clients. In so doing, it makes a brand—or personality—statement. The consulting firm may also have a fancy phone system that speaks of financial success but can be off-putting to a mom-and-pop shop needing consulting services.

If we agree that the brand possesses an attitude about its customers, then organizations must consider how to manage the brand's attitudes. For example, customer segmentation (dividing customers into groups primarily based on volume of business) can create an attitude that is delivered behaviorally and says in effect, "You won't get such great treatment from us because you don't give us much business." For service companies, this segmentation is manifested in large part through staff behavior.

Airlines have to be very cautious about this. If they provide great treatment only for their most frequent flyers, there is very little incentive for low-mileage passengers to concentrate their miles with that airline. As frequent travelers, we both notice that when we are not on our preferred airlines we are treated as if we have lesser value. No airline advertises itself this way, but the staff behave this way. It's off-brand behavior.

While branding once was seen as one-way communication from an organization to consumers, today branding is viewed as interactive communication. That is, incidentally, exactly what branded customer service is. Today's brands are presented as groups of ideas, rather than merely logos. As such, they have lost their tight legal definitions and have come to represent an almost human way for organizations to communicate with the public. Part of that communication includes even the chatter that goes on inside the organization itself.[23]

Are brands losing their power to attract?

Some have suggested that consumers today are more apathetic toward brands than in the past, and there is at least scattered evidence to support the notion. Brand loyalty in the financial industry, for example, as reported by the Carlson Marketing Company, decreased by 25 percent between 2000 and 2001. This is a particularly strong trend with the important under-thirty-five age group.[24] The reputable PIMS research organization reports that in the year 2000, four out of ten consumers in the UK described themselves as having a genuine preference for branded merchandise. By 2001, that number had slipped to three in ten.[25]

Fortune magazine also reports an earthquake occurring in consumer product brands that is shaking the marketer's world: "Retailers—once the lowly peddlers of brands that were made and marketed by big, important manufacturers—are now behaving like full-fledged marketers."[26] And the private-label brands are winning market share. It should be pointed out, however, that in these situations, one brand category is winning over another. This is brand warfare, not that brands themselves are losing.

One reason that perhaps explains brand slippage is that branding used to differentiate quality. Today's product quality, however, has dramatically improved everywhere. Even fakes churned out in Asia are largely indistinguishable in quality from the famous European brands they copy. As Brian Kardon, with Cahners Business Information, says, "Quality itself is a commodity in the consumers' eyes—it's easy to get. It's the price of entry."[27] As a result, unless brands are distinguished on something other than product quality, many of today's consumers are not likely to remain loyal to their brands.

Brand identity

Brand identities, such as that enjoyed by Starship, create anticipation in the minds of both consumers who use the brand and the employees who deliver it. The strongest brands tend to be the ones with the most consistent and clearest messages. A strong brand character, according to Mark Kingsbury of Research International, provides the following benefits: "Consumers know how to 'connect' with a brand that has character, they know what it stands for and they also know what it's not trying to be."[28]

A brand with character can never be all things to all people. This is a critical point. Successful brands do not appeal to everyone. Rather they reflect specific benefits or experiences that engage the hearts and minds of a discrete, targeted segment of consumers. Whether the segment is narrow or wide, a strong brand's identity is shaped around the unique alignment between "what we offer" and the identified consumer group's needs, aspirations, and preferences. Once the nuances of this relationship are understood and the brand is defined, the consistency of reinforcing advertising, packaging, endorsements, and *customer service* begins to build the relationship between the brand and the customer.

Brand identity feelings are primarily unconscious. Estimated to be as much as 95 percent below conscious awareness,[29] these feelings and judgments operate very quickly—much more quickly than conscious evaluation.[30] Harvard professor Gerald Zaltman relates the unlikely example of a manufacturer of paints, a commodity product. The organization discovered that purchasing agents were willing to pay premium prices for branded paint when salespeople linked self-esteem to the sale.[31] Zaltman notes that marketing researchers typically overlook the emotional benefits of brands, focusing 90 percent of their research on the functional benefits of products or services.[32]

This quick unconscious mental processing of such feelings impacts most of our consumer choices—even our entertainment choices. Julia Roberts has been the highest paid female star for twenty years, in great part because movie fans know if they see one of her movies they will walk away feeling good. It is a decision they do not have to think through when choosing which movie to see.

That feeling can be security: *I made a good choice.* It possibly is superiority: *I know how to make good choices. I know value or quality when I see it.* It might be excitement: *I had a great time!* It could also be a feeling of genuine, high value that will be long lasting: *I was moved by that film.* It possibly is relief: *Now I can tell everyone I saw it, too!* All variations of these judgments are held in the minds of customers, helping them make choices, define who they are, and simply get them through their days.

Brand stories

Brand stories broaden and deepen the brand concept even further by relating memorable examples to human concerns, aspirations, and emotions. The stories point to a possible future. Ideally, brand stories capture both the essence of the past *and* a yearning for the future.

Brand stories not only provide inspiration for customers but also provide motivation and direction for staff.

A good brand story tells the truth about an organization—if not today's truth, then a truth that is aspired to. Successful brands incorporate good stories. A tagline on a brand, such as Nike's "Just do it," can begin to tell the story. But it is just a beginning. If the tagline does not match staff behavior, then a great deal of the service an organization delivers will be seen as off-brand.

An important aspect of a brand story is that it be consistent with everything the company does. To a large degree, customers return because they believe that what they bought last week (products, experiences, and feelings) is still available today. Brand stories are assets of an organization because they generate pride and inspire staff. They show staff how it is possible to deliver the brand.

ARAMARK Harrison Lodging, whose brand promise is customer focus at all levels of its operation, has several such brand stories. A guest showed up at one of Harrison Lodging's conference centers looking a little dejected. When the front desk clerk asked if anything was wrong, the man, who had just flown in, said he had left his antique copy of an Edgar Allan Poe book on the airplane. To make matters worse, he had read only to chapter 4! The clerk took it upon herself the next day to go to a close-by antique bookshop to see if the book was available. She found it, purchased it, and placed it in the guest's room—with a bookmark deftly placed at chapter 4.

The by-product of this approach to service (when staff are imbued in the brand story, committed to delivering its promise, and empowered to do so) is that more often than not, staff will aim to excel and will find the experience of service delivery far more stimulating. The customer will feel this as well. And the brand will be remembered for its attributes—in ARAMARK Harrison Lodging's case, "customer focus."

on-brand

We recently heard a speaker discuss his strange penchant for not fastening his seat belt upon plane takeoffs. He said that most flight attendants let him know in no uncertain terms to buckle his seat belt. In contrast, on Southwest Airlines (the successfully branded high-spirited and fun airline), a flight attendant came up to him and said, "Whoops, look at that! Your seat belt is in two pieces!"

Therein lies the magic of brand Southwest Airlines—fun and love.

Strong brands make economic sense

Top-rated brands invariably capture larger market share. In part, their sheer size feeds their growth. This is why branding is such a hot topic today. Strong brands are incredibly valuable and profitable, and once at the top of the list, they tend to remain there. It all comes down to making a customer eager and happy to pay over a hundred dollars for a white cotton T-shirt with the costly German brand "Escada" printed on it in small rhinestones, compared to an identical unbranded T-shirt that might seem overpriced at $14.95.

The following statistics are pulled from a variety of sources, and they all point to the same conclusion: strong brands make economic sense.

Customers pay higher prices and get more involved with brands they love.

- Harley-Davidson's branding has created HOG (Harley Owners Group), a club with 750,000 members, many who have the HOG brand tattooed on their bodies! They pay $40 annually to have a strong taste of the Harley-Davidson experience.[33]
- Customers will pay 19 percent more for a leading brand name as compared to a weak brand.[34]

- Eighteen percent of a consumer's decision to purchase is determined by brand issues.[35]
- Once consumers buy a branded product or service, they become more aware of the brand's advertising. This, in turn, leads to more sales. That first buy is critical for the brand.[36]

Strong brands impact stock prices and profitability.

- Strong brands command stock prices between 5 and 7 percent higher than weak brands.[37]
- Tangible assets of a typical organization today are evaluated to comprise a mere 25 percent of the value of an organization. This is a big switch from thirty years ago. John Murphy, a UK branding guru, points out that tangible assets used to make up 80 percent of the value of a company, though he admits that valuing brand equity is "an altogether imprecise science." During the 1990s, brand assets (patent rights, intellectual property, copyright and other trademarks) were valued at 75 percent.[38] In the late 1990s, the book value of Coca-Cola (the number one brand in the world) was less than 10 percent of its total value. In other words, 90 percent of Coca-Cola's value is intangible, most of it coming from the brand itself.[39]
- Investors, too, are becoming much more concerned about this issue, placing increased emphasis on strategies around intangible values, such as brand and customer loyalty. In a series of studies of UK institutional investors through the 1990s, Brand Finance, a leading independent brand valuation agency, found that the importance placed on branding increases every year. And over 70 percent of investors demand more information from companies regarding their brand strength and values.[40]

Strong brands have more loyal customers and staff.

- Companies with customer loyalty rates that are above average enjoy a price-to-earnings ratio twice that of competitors'.[41] Perhaps because of this, customer loyalty is the highest ranking topic that CEOs think and worry about.[42]

- More employees stay with a company when the company lives its brand internally, and this impacts profit margins. Frederick Reichheld found that fast-food stores with lower employee turnover (the average in the fast-food industry is 100 percent!) have profit margins 50 percent higher when compared to stores with 150 percent staff turnover.[43]

- "Strong brands more easily leverage selling efforts into sales success" is an idea supported by a study on institutional brand perceptions and marketing effectiveness. For money managers who are affiliated with branded financial institutions, this makes prospects more likely to become clients.[44]

- Even though some in-store brands are taking market share away from the big national brands, study after study reveals that consumers trust branded FMCG products more than they trust private store brands. For example, in data that crosses national lines, consumers indicate that they trust branded pet foods by over 50 percent when compared to private store brands.[45]

- A brand that is number one in its category is trusted at significantly higher degrees than the second, third, or smaller brands in a product category. Consumers also believe that the top-ranked brand—regardless of the product or service—cares more about its customers, stands for family values, and produces wholesome products.[46]

- Brand leaders have disproportionately higher brand preference and loyalty than that achieved by the weaker brands. For example, a brand with twice the brand recognition will typically command three to four times the brand preference and loyalty of competitors.[47]

If all or even a portion of the above statistics are accurate—and the people who have created them will certainly attest to the robust nature of their brand research—then integrated brand development is a strategic driver that organizations cannot ignore. In short, magnifying the strength of brands with aligned customer service delivery is a solid business decision.

Brand study: Apple Computer claims its defined space

Janelle feels strongly about her computer brand, Macintosh. To be more accurate, she should say her Apples, for she has several. Are Macintosh products of a higher quality than PCs? Janelle does not really know, even though Apple's core message is "insanely great computers." Certainly if all one does is look at market share, the Macintosh brand isn't doing very well. Yet Apple was just named as the world's second most impactful brand in a survey by Interbrand, after first place Google, the wildly popular Internet search engine.[48]

There seems to be little question that if Apple were not so strongly branded, it would not exist. The PC market would have eaten it for lunch, but Apple maintains itself. Many of Apple's early competitors, such as Osborn, Kaypro, Commodore, and Atari, no longer exist.

Here's how columnist Mark Morford raved about the latest Apple products:

> Apple actually cares about (design). Which is odd. Which is rare. Which is why they deserve gushing adulation now and then. They actually put the time and energy and labor into creating a gorgeous package most people will toss anyway, and why they include a first-time welcome experience, with subtle music, with flowing lush clean graphics, one that will never be repeated, just because.
>
> This is the point. Detail and nuance and texture and a sense of how users actually feel, what makes them smile, what makes the experience

worthy and positive and sensual instead of necessary and drab and evil.[49]

When the first Macintosh was introduced, the brand was defined as "computers for the rest of us." People said that when you took a Mac home with you, it wasn't a one-night stand. It was a love affair. As Jonathan Ive, designer of the latest line of Macs, says, "People smile when they see an IMAC." Apple went down in branding history with its 1984 Super Bowl commercial showing a woman athlete freeing the IBM-shackled drones by hurling a sledgehammer through Big Blue's video image. Apple paid to show that lengthy commercial only once, yet it continues to get air play even today. It set a tone about the company that has endured.[50]

Most lovers of the Macintosh brand display a special feeling and passion that PC users simply do not have. Their reaction is explained by Professor Gerald Zaltman at Harvard Business School: "Consumer preferences and motivation are far less influenced by the functional attributes of products and services than the subconscious sensory and emotional elements derived by the total experience."[51] And Apple has been providing strong experiences for decades.

People who are loyal to the Macintosh brand notice and appreciate that other Apple users feel the same way. They are an informal club that you never have to join to be a member.[52] Members of this club love it when they are in an audience and the presenter asks who is a Mac user. Apple users practically leap out of their chairs in an effort to raise their hands. They are normally thrilled when someone notices the distinctive partially eaten apple that adorns the front of their laptops. And Apple aficionados were all very happy when the Apple corporation began to pull itself out of its slump. For a period of time, many committed Apple users, while they rather relish their minority status, were secretly worried that their beloved Apples were no longer going to be available.

CEO Steve Jobs has managed to convey a strong sense of rebellion around the Apple brand. He even rode back in his blue jeans and black turtleneck sweater to rescue the company. In many ways, Jobs is the Apple brand. Certainly he personifies it, which helps to reinforce its edgy image. This positioning seems to be strategic as Apple extends the brand with iPods and other products.

The challenge of channel marketing

Like Harley-Davidson, the Apple company enjoys the luxury of having users who engage in on-brand behavior with each other. Most users discuss their Apples only in the most glowing terms. However, when customers get involved with representatives (salespeople or service providers) of such strong product brands, matters can become so much more complicated.

Some of Apple's channel distributors do not have adequate product knowledge to sell the Mac. For example, Fry's Electronics, the gigantic American high-tech retailer, carries a full range of Apple products. Its salespeople, however, do not express the same enthusiastic attitude about the equipment that you experience when you shop at an Apple store. Janelle was recently referred to Fry's resident "Apple guru." This guru's qualification was that he once owned an old model Mac.

It is a lot to ask of service representatives, but if the Apple corporation were to take full advantage of its brand proposition ("insanely great computers"), every person who spoke for Apple would display the same consistent degree of style, excitement, and user-friendliness. After all, if customers feel this way about their Macs, why shouldn't the people who sell and service them feel the same way?

We talked with the marketing director of a large high-tech company that sells a high percentage of its products through marketing channels. When we asked about how the company manages the brand through its distributors, he responded rather flippantly, "We don't consider their customers our customers." We think this is a big mistake, a huge wasted brand opportunity.

Professor Zaltman cautions against such an approach as he considers the power of accumulated social memory and customer interactions regardless of how the customer experiences the product or service:

> People who manage customer relationships must grasp how consumers store, retrieve, and reconstruct memories of every interaction with a firm. These interactions may be direct, as when customers deal with a global account manager. They may also be indirect, as through word-of-mouth. And every new encounter alters a customer's recall of a prior encounter—often in trivial ways, but sometimes in significant ways. Thus every customer interaction can make—or break—a brand.[53]

Most people who buy Morton Salt will never meet a representative of the Morton company. And they do not spend a lot of time discussing salt with their neighbors. Avid fans of Diet Coke will probably never get any closer to the Coca-Cola Company than to visit the Coke Museum or to read a book or magazine article about the corporation. This is not the case with most high-tech products. People discuss their computers and software, and toll-free (or charged) support lines represent the high-tech brands as much as styling and functionality elements.

Since the introduction of Apple's new OSX operating system, our personal experience with Apple's direct telephone support is that it is largely on-brand. Apple technicians talk about the new products with great love, "Ooh, you have the newest G4. I'd give anything to have one of those." One technician raved about the beautiful *interiors* of the new G5. Janelle spoke to a technical representative after she bought the new seventeen-inch Apple Powerbook and the technician began to sing "Happy Days Are Here Again"—awesome, on-brand reinforcement! In a PC-dominated world, Apple's survival alone is miraculous and speaks to the power of carefully crafted branding.

2

Generic Customer Service Isn't Enough Anymore

A few years ago, Janelle saw an ad on television about a new product the Postal Service was offering—a mailing option called International Priority Mail. It was a takeoff on the immensely popular domestic Priority Mail product the Postal Service successfully created to compete with the higher prices of UPS and Federal Express.

The ad was compelling. It showed a spirited customer walking up to the counter of a brand new, spotlessly clean post office where a beautiful young blond-haired woman stood with a charming and big welcoming smile on her face. Regally perched on her shoulder was an American bald eagle. The "clerk," whose perfect teeth flashed behind her smile, took the customer's package and placed it into the eagle's beak, and off it flew into the distance. Old Glory fluttered in the wind accompanied by patriotic music playing in the background. At least this is how Janelle remembered it.

She was both captivated and impressed! Furthermore, if International Priority Mail worked as well as domestic Priority Mail, she was willing to give her next international letter to that eagle.

Two days later Janelle drove to her local post office, international letter in hand. The post office she walked into did not look quite like the new one in the advertisement. And the woman behind the counter, with no eagle on her shoulder, did not quite look like the fair young beauty in the commercial, either. However, Janelle understands that ads must sell a best face to the customer, and the main message of the ad was that the post office is reasonably priced and, therefore, a logical shipping alternative to UPS and FedEx.

After a lengthy wait in line, Janelle walked up to the counter with an anticipatory smile on her face and said, "I'd like to try your new service, International Priority Mail." The clerk inspected her fingernails, looked at Janelle, and announced, "It ain't cheap."

Organizations spend millions to tell the world how they would like consumers to think about their brand offerings, and then a human being with three simple words can shatter the illusion. One could argue that Janelle actually received good generic service at the post office. At least the clerk seemed to be offering advice that there might be a less expensive way to send her package around the world. That type of information provides value to customers. But one thing we know for sure: "It ain't cheap" flies straight in the face of the Postal Service's new product positioning as a reasonably priced alternative. It is safe to bet that the Postal Service did little or nothing to appropriately prepare its thousands of staff to be on-brand for the influx of customers coming to try out its new product.

Brands deliver customers; being on-brand keeps them coming back

A strong brand has power in that it motivates customers toward a positive response or specific action. The Postal Service's television ad on International Priority Mail appealed to Janelle at both these levels and delivered her to the post office to try the new product. This is the positive end result of successful marketing efforts. Some marketing specialists, in fact, live by the premise that perception is reality and that a well-constructed brand promise can be the basis for such a strong and compelling advertising image that nonaligned service delivery can be overlooked.

We have seen many firsthand examples of companies that clearly, and quite intentionally, promised something they were in no position to deliver in the near future. The belief that an organization can acquire market space simply by creating perceptual leads is pervasive in some industries, particularly the fast-moving technology sector. Many high-tech companies appear to have a strategy of capturing customers through exaggerated advertising and sales promises. They hope customers will remain loyal after they have purchased—regardless of how far the company is from delivering what it has enticingly promised. As someone wryly pointed out, "Microsoft does its beta testing on the whole world's population!" Unfortunately, since so many of the giant technology companies do this, the public is forced to endure it.

We agree that a strong brand promise can influence what customers remember about their experiences with a product or service. However, this well-documented advertising placebo effect can be easily overridden by negative service experiences. New product introductions must be managed very delicately or they may severely compromise trust and integrity in the brand and produce customers who fully understand the advice "Buyer beware." Such marketing disasters also create cynical, dissonant employees.

The automotive industry has struggled to get dealers to deliver the experiences they hint at in their emotionally appealing advertising. Shopping for a car should be a lot of fun since there is nothing quite like the thrill of owning a new car. Yet for many people, going through the process is painful. Many women never do it primarily because of the way they are treated.

Saturn has achieved a high degree of success in its attempts to brand itself as a car company that offers a different shopping experience. It has done this by first understanding the market segment it wants to attract, then designing a brand look and advertising to support the message, and finally reinforcing an unusual brand promise through its service delivery.

One of Saturn's most striking brand pledges is "hassle free." To Saturn this means you will not have to haggle over prices or wonder if someone who bought a car two hours before you got a better price because he or she bargained with the dealer. Here is how Saturn describes its brand promise on its Web page:

> Creating a "No-Hassle, No-Haggle" sales policy wasn't intended to create a revolution, just to solve a problem. We don't like getting the runaround any more than you do, which is why we set out to be honest and straightforward with our customers. We just thought it was a good idea and that if there were more people out there like us, we'd do okay. Turns out, we were right. Over the years, consumer research has shown repeatedly that our customers rate Saturn top in sales satisfaction.

Good thinking on Saturn's part! The Gallup Organization, the polling company, reports that customers are ten to fifteen times more likely to buy their next brand of car from a specific dealer if they perceive that dealer to be different from "all the other dealers."[1] Even if buying a car is a good experience, if it is generic and undistinguishable, it will do little to enhance a specific brand image. "Different from all others," such as a guaranteed no-haggle sales policy, is brand reinforcing—especially when it is delivered so customers can count on it as part of their service experience.

The heart of the challenge: delivering brands through service experiences

The most successful brands in the world, most of which are product brands, are tightly managed. By employing precise guidelines, marketers find it comparatively easy to manage consumer brands such as Coca-Cola, Colgate toothpaste, or Bayer aspirin. Assuring that a consistent container of Coca-Cola will end up in the consumers' hands, however, is considerably different than guaranteeing what will happen when customers and service providers have either direct or indirect contact.

A classic case is Morton Salt, the epitome of an FMCG. It has a strong brand character appealing to tradition, quality, and goodness and is offered with minimal service interaction. Salt is pretty much salt. Yet American consumers buy Morton Salt more than any other, primarily because people trust the character of the brand. Salt is a textbook example of a commodity. In this fast-changing world, even brands that are commodities can provide continuity in consumers' lives.[2] Most American families (Morton Salt was founded in 1848) grew up with the image of Morton's little girl, her umbrella, and free-flowing salt. Brands can become so strongly associated with events and people, such as childhood and our mothers, that we can literally feel the spirit of another person every time we engage the brand.[3]

Most consumers never have problems with Morton Salt, nor do they have to meet with representatives of Morton Salt who might challenge their experience of the brand. Grocery-store shoppers appreciate not having to decide which brand of salt to buy, even though they basically are all the same. When consumers make a salt purchasing decision at the end of a long day at work, their harried brains do not have to ponder which brand to purchase. In this world of seemingly endless choices, consumers appreciate this as well. And they are willing to pay a bit more for Morton to have that feeling of ease, security, and emotional connection with their past sitting in their kitchen cupboards.

When humans get involved with delivering service brands, meeting expectations created by advertising is far more difficult to guarantee. Controlling human service interactions, because of their dynamism, richness, and uniqueness, can be quite elusive. This is the key challenge for companies with products that have a high degree of customer service contact (software, automotive, telecommunication, hospitality, or airline companies) or whose product line is delivered exclusively through people (accounting, medical, legal, or publishing companies).

You can reinforce a brand idea, making it stronger with pictures, language, and behaviors—all of which evoke emotion. Human behavior is the primary means of brand reinforcement within the realm of customer service. It is easy for us to underestimate the impact of brands delivered by "collections of people joined together in pursuit of a common cause, and it is people who create value," as stated by brand expert Nicholas Ind.[4]

When service representatives and customers dance together in brand space, it is difficult to predict or control what will happen. As Rod Oram, a leading New Zealand business commentator, underscored in discussions with us about this topic, "It is relatively easy to design and make the perfect product in the controlled environment of a factory, but it is immensely harder to deliver perfect service in the incredibly random, unpredictable environment of customer service."

How can an organization meet the expectations of a tightly defined brand proposition but within the context of the very personal and individual experience that is customer service? This is the crux of the challenge and it again brings to mind the red-billed quelea flying in gigantic flocks, engaging in organized behavior while maintaining individual form.

What you see through a service lens is what you deliver

If you place a branded service lens in front of your organization, you make it easier for your staff to evaluate whether they are on-brand or off-brand. Contrast this with a generic service lens approach where the service staff look at customers through the lens of satisfaction. Then the service standard becomes, Did I offer good service or bad service? The lens through which your staff evaluate their service delivery drives their behavior.

The "customer satisfaction" lens produces behavior tending to gravitate to the ordinary, i.e., delivering the same generic service standard as competitors—and honestly believing that is good enough. Viewing service through a branded service lens amplifies branded service uniqueness. The questions staff ask become: Did I create a brand experience for my customers? Did I reinforce our brand? Did I deliver on our brand promise? Behind these questions lies the most powerful latent question: Am I creating brand loyalty among the customers we are targeting?

---

off-brand

A subscriber to the Best of Active Learning (Singapore-based Ron Kaufman's e-letter that goes out to thirty-five thousand people) wrote about his experience with a cruise line that promotes itself on the basis of exclusivity and personalization that was not entirely on-brand in his estimation. Here's what the customer experienced:

> *The cruise company worked hard to personalize the vacation for each individual on board. Precruise telephone calls and letters identified each traveler's likes and dislikes, hopes, dreams (and concerns, if any) regarding the upcoming voyage.*
>
> *On the ship, the entire staff made a huge effort to memorize every passenger's name. Personal preferences were rigorously recorded and used to upgrade the intimacy of service each day. On the final morning, a questionnaire was slipped under the door of every cabin asking for feedback and suggestions for improvement. The first three questions on the form were:*

An entire cruise devoted to impeccable, personal service on a cruise line that is branded for personalized unique service. And one "standard form" at the end of the cruise reminds the guests they are merely anonymous respondents.[5]

The above situation, like so many service experiences, is a subtle example of off-brand service. Asking people to write their names on an evaluation form is definitely not bad service. Some might even prefer it so their feedback can remain anonymous. However, it is definitely off-brand when it comes from a cruise line that stakes its reputation on extreme personalized service.

Some passengers probably would not even notice this disparity. Nonetheless, at one of its final customer touch points, which are the most vivid and memorable in service experiences, the cruise line lost a last opportunity to reinforce its brand.[6] This is an outstanding cruise line. It's the same cruise line whose staff notice when you leave cashews in your cocktail nut dish so the next time you are served nuts, you will receive not a single cashew. And, of course, one passenger clearly noted the disparity about the evaluation form and experienced enough brand erosion to write about it to a newsletter with an enormous circulation.

Based on considerable research, we know that satisfaction is not enough to drive customer loyalty, making it a poor lens through which to evaluate service. A recent consumer survey, for example, indicates that the most common descriptor consumers use to describe the service they receive is "satisfied."[7] Professor Michael Edwardson, with the University of New South Wales and one of the authors of that survey, suggests that "satisfaction" is meaningless because even dissatisfied people will say they are satisfied. When consumers say they are satisfied, Edwardson concludes, it means nothing significant happened. In fact, he states that we have "taught" consumers to say they are satisfied when they fill out survey forms.[8]

Service moments of truth through the eyes of branding

Ever since Jan Carlzon, former CEO of Scandinavian Airlines, wrote a book called *Moments of Truth,* the phrase has become de rigueur in customer service.[9] It has come to mean those defining moments when customers evaluate products and services and pronounce "This is good" or "I don't like this." Industries, such as the hospitality industry with many complex customer interactions, can have thousands of moments of truth every day.

The term has become so integrated into customer service language that many do not know it originated in bullfighting. It is that critical point in the bullfight when the matador faces the bull in the defining moment of truth: is the matador going to defeat the bull or be defeated? Through arduous training, matadors have been trained for their precise moments of truth. They know exactly what to do. They seldom lose, rarely are even injured, though fighting live, angry bulls is admittedly dangerous work. Matadors clearly understand the essence of their moments of truth. They have pictured just about everything that can happen and behave precisely with those pictures in mind, or they are matadors no longer.

Unfortunately, too many organizations simply put their customer-facing staff into the service ring without an ounce of brand training. At best, they receive generic service training that many refer to as "smile training." Most organizations assume that people who interact with customers are knowledgeable about basic human interaction and will therefore intuit the appropriate way to behave toward customers. That could be the situation if your aspiration is simply good generic service, but there is no way to intuit appropriate on-brand behaviors without at least rudimentary brand knowledge. Since, in many cases, employees do not even know what the brand message is, through no fault of their own they simply do not have enough information to deliver branded service.

And who do you suppose notices that? Who do you suppose is experiencing that off-brand moment of truth? Kevin Roberts, CEO Worldwide of Saatchi & Saatchi, the well-branded advertising agency, talks of two moments of truth: when consumers choose and when they use.[10] If marketing promises something specific to consumers, the organization needs to be as concerned about what happens during service interactions as when customers turn on their televisions in the morning and watch ads.

off-brand

Dave Ratner, owner of Dave's Soda and Pet City in Massachusetts, saw an ad by Tweeter that emphasized its staff's "boatload of knowledge." He needed a minidisc player and walked into a Tweeter HiFi Buys store wanting to take advantage of that knowledge. "Hi, I want to buy a minidisc player and accessories if somebody can show me how to use it." He was told, "I don't know how it's used, but they're supposed to be really easy." Dave says, "The boatload of knowledge just capsized."

If you visit the Tweeter Web site, it is filled with plenty of aspirational statements about the intelligence and knowledgeability of the staff. ("Expert Salespeople. Our salespeople are dedicated professionals, highly trained experts on the equipment who use plain language and guide you toward the right decision.") Its opening graphic, "We love this stuff!" speaks to an intense involvement with the products that the salesman Dave Ratner ran into obviously did not have on his boat.

Moments of truth are particularly important for new customers. A customer who has been to Tweeter several times might excuse one staff worker who is clearly lacking a boatload of knowledge, but a first-time customer can be turned off permanently by a single experience that contradicts the expectation created through brand marketing.[11]

The swell of customer dissatisfaction

Dissatisfaction with customer service is burgeoning. Not only is this discontent reflected in many nationwide and individual organizational surveys, but now this grumbling is also the talk of the Internet with entire Web sites devoted to attacking different brands.

Even as businesses struggle to improve their customer service and top management aims at a strong brand, we are regaled by many telling us that service is horrible, that service is getting worse, and that service standards have fallen. Some claim that the current generation of people getting ready to enter the job market has learned neither manners nor any of the basic ingredients of service.

And today, with the Internet and twenty-four-hour news television stations, a single negative incident can be multiplied and dispensed rapidly to send a company's stock and brand name plummeting. Perhaps the best example of this was what happened to UK jewelry chain store owner Gerald Ratner. Admittedly, Ratner was known for his "loose lips," but in a 1991 speech to the Institute of Directors, his words sank the ship of his brand. Ratner, certainly in a moment he came to regret, proclaimed that the jewelry sold at H. Samuels and Ernst Jones, owned by the Ratner Group, was "total crap." The Ratner Group's share price slumped 96 percent, and the company fell from huge profitability to massive losses in one short year. The brand Ratner had invested in for so long was destroyed, and he was subsequently forced out of the business. The press damage was so severe that the group later renamed itself Signet and the process of building a new brand started from scratch.[12]

Virus-like, word-of-mouth complaining on the Web can be enormously damaging to brands. A disgruntled Doubletree Hotels customer recently created an engaging PowerPoint presentation that has been circulated widely as an e-mail attachment.[13] The customer, arriving late at night, was denied a room that had been guaranteed with his credit card—not delivering Doubletree's tagline, "Relax, You're Among Friends." It demonstrates the shuddering impact of brand bashing caused by the behavior of one employee and responded to by one customer.

One major cause of brand slippage is simple, in our estimation, but normally overlooked in the rush to develop a strong brand. Many branding agencies, and the companies for whom these brands are created, are so focused on the physical product and articulation of the product's brand promise that they pay inadequate attention to (or forget about or overlook or choose to ignore or are afraid of addressing) the largest part of the delivery system of a service brand—namely, the interaction service providers have directly with customers.

Paul recently worked with a large company to develop a complaint-handling workshop. After meeting with the marketing department, he suggested building the workshop content around the new brand position that was about to be launched in a nationwide television campaign. The relief expressed by the marketers was almost overwhelming. They knew the organization's service needed to be aligned with the brand and the new advertising campaign, but they simply did not have the time or resources to do anything about it and meet their own deadlines. The need to grab new customers was given greater priority by the executive team than ensuring that new and existing customers would experience what they had been promised.

When products have services attached to them, advertising sets expectations prior to customers' interaction with the organization. Then treatment of customers becomes the key factor in judgments of the brand. The fourteen-year-old daughter of one of TMI's staff behaves as a typical teenager in relationship to branded products. Kelly Fedderson and her friends are enticed by ads in teen magazines. But their product loyalty is primarily based on treatment they receive from store clerks that sell the branded products they think are "cool." In Kelly's words: "MAC was one of the makeup lines we used to love. The people behind the counters look so edgy, so radical. But when we were waiting in line, the clerks looked right past us—like we weren't there! They started to serve other people first just because they were older! We were so embarrassed."

Without trust in your brand, forget it!

A product or service is just an aspect of a brand—in some cases perhaps not the most important part of the brand experience. The ways products or services are displayed, talked about, and handled and problems are solved all relate to trust and the total brand experience. And when customer service delivery and products are aligned so the brand can be trusted, the effect is irresistible. When not, the impact is palpable and memorable.

---

on-brand *and* off-brand

Janelle and her husband live in the Red Rock Country Club community in Las Vegas. Here is how the Web site promotes the community: "Welcome to Red Rock Country Club. Live Exclusive. Play Private."

After extensive travel, Janelle returned to the club and was greeted by a young woman behind the counter, "Dr. Barlow! You're back! We missed you." She received an exclusive greeting using a formal title yet with a very personal welcome. It was decidedly on-brand, creating a strong feeling of belonging.

Yet when Janelle repeatedly complained about the temperature of the Club's lap pool that was being kept at a temperature higher than advertised, she was told among other things by the general manager, "Look, lady, you're not the only one who swims in that pool,"—not exactly "live exclusive" or "play private." It felt more like feedback one might receive at a public swimming pool. It was definitely off-brand, making it impossible for Janelle to trust the quality of her morning swim and how she will be treated when complaining about it.

Consumers ask: Can I trust this organization? Are promises met when it actually delivers its products and services? Is it following through on commitments, or is its advertising just so many words and images with no action behind them? Clearly, a company's ability to deliver what it declares is fundamental to its reputation. Therefore, the ability to move from a compelling strategy about a brand to authentic delivery of the brand is paramount in building trust.

We know that trust is hard to come by in today's world, as witnessed by deceptions from a growing list of our most revered institutions. A recent study put a large exclamation mark on this point. Sponsored by the respected Society of Consumer Affairs Professionals, four thousand customers of nine blue-chip Australian organizations were surveyed. The study revealed that only one in twenty customers trust the organizations that serve them; even worse, only one in forty believe organizations trust them![14]

You can say "trust me," but that does not mean you are trustworthy. Food giants Kellogg and Cadbury are more trusted in the UK than either the police force or the British government. Yet both the police and government regularly insist they are trustworthy.[15] Since trust is formed as a result of the judgments people make about behaviors over a period of time, developing a brand is much like establishing the character of a person. Consumers have learned through experience that Kellogg and Cadbury deliver consistent quality and products that speak to them personally, thereby proving they can be trusted. Apparently this is lacking with British law enforcement and government burdened with the challenge of delivering service through staff.

If you are to achieve the type of customer-staff interaction that enhances your brand, you must offer more than lip service to the value of trust. Branding can be best understood as a business strategy in great part to gain consumer trust. In this regard, branding is like broad market satisfaction and trust development, both of which have long been regarded by marketing experts as "relatively stable, cumulative phenomena that change gradually over time."[16]

Branding strategy needs to be looked at in terms of its long-term market impact. If you want to get into the marketplace, make some quick revenue, and then get out, then branding is not for you. Branding is more transformational in terms of how it ultimately shapes organizations precisely because it is trust based: we promise, we deliver. When this is not done, customer relationships are more likely to be short-term, immediate, and transactional—and do little to build brand trust.

Jack Welch, former CEO of General Electric, underscores the uneasy nature of any transformational strategy that is put into place—and then must be allowed to proceed on its own: "The essence of competitiveness is liberated when we make people believe that what they think and do is important—and then get out of their way while they do it."[17]

You need to equip your customer service representatives with information, tools, techniques, and ideas that assist in creating positive customer transactions. Equally important, you must imbue them with the "fragrance" of your brand and then "get out of their way" so they can deliver. Only then will staff be encouraged to use their best judgment as to what is required to deliver the brand in each unique customer exchange and thereby develop consumer trust.

Trustworthy does not mean merely being reliable. Based on Research International's studies, brand trust has much more to do with intimacy; that is, how does the organization show customers they are more than just statistics, that it knows them personally?[18]

---

off-brand   NO TRUST

Janelle recently went to her HMO to pick up a drug prescription from a doctor who was staffing the evening clinic. Janelle had been promised a prescription from her regular physician, but his office had failed to send it to the pharmacy (Trust Violation No. 1). Janelle was leaving the United States the next morning, so she went to the after-hours clinic. The emergency doctor insisted on doing all types of tests, including taking her temperature and weighing her, when all she wanted was a prescription that had been promised earlier in the day over the phone. When Janelle protested, the doctor said, "How can I trust you? I don't know you" (Trust Violation No. 2). Janelle responded, "How can you not know or trust me? I've been a member of your health services for two and a half years. You have my complete medical records in front of you that show I have been taking this medication for the entire time period."

The impact of customer contact on loyalty

Numerous studies have demonstrated the links between advertising, brand strength, and financial performance. Without the strong quantifiable results of these studies, organizations would not be likely to invest so much money in advertising. A brand that holds a leadership position in its product or service category delivers superior profitability. This profitability provides an opportunity to extend brand leadership through more advertising and investment of capital in acquisitions, product development, and customer service. But research also shows that brand dominance is greatest for products and services where regularity of contact with salespeople is low.[19] This disparity implies that the more regular the contact the consumer has with sales or service staff, the more likely the brand will not be delivered in that service contact.

David Burrows with TDA (The Design Agency) in England says that "40 percent of marketing investment is wasted, as ill-informed or demotivated behavior by staff unwittingly undermines the promotional promise. The result is that 68 percent of those who do buy go away because of how they were treated."[20]

Customer service can be your ongoing brand reinforcer

Firsthand experience strongly influences consumers about repurchase decisions. In other words, customers become primed by every experience to create more positive memories of earlier brand experiences. Based on their research, Richard Elliot and Kritsadarat Wattanasuwan at Oxford University in England conclude, "lived experience with a brand, through purchase and usage over the life cycle, will tend to dominate the mediated experience of advertising."[21] Reinforcing a brand through every customer touch point, therefore, can provide the repetition necessary to inspire repeat purchasing decisions.

Indeed, the Gallup Organization polled six thousand passengers and discovered that, by a ratio of between three and four to one, employees of airlines are *more important* than advertising messages in building brand loyalty. Banking customers are ten to twenty times more likely to return if the organization has outstanding employees. And in the telecommunications industry, the loyalty of customers is influenced by employees of the organization at a ratio of between three and five to one, compared to advertising.[22]

Loyalty is behavior that grows out of an ongoing relationship

Advertising may start the flame of attraction to a brand, but reinforcing service experiences fuel the relationship. Figure 2 shows the relationship between the dynamics of advertising, service interactions, and levels of brand loyalty.[23] Brand loyalty starts with awareness of the company and its products. "Let's give them a try," no doubt, is initiated mainly through some type of advertising or word of mouth. This leads to a desire to purchase products or services. Once a purchase has been made, as the chart below indicates, a positive brand reinforcing experience will strengthen the consumer's feeling of engagement. This reduces the requirement that advertising be the only driver of further purchasing behaviors.

Many companies have invested millions in CRM (customer relationship management) technology to build customer loyalty. But CRM is merely a tool. The essence of human interaction is fundamental for demonstrating who you are to customers. Nonetheless, hundreds of puzzled organizational leaders are wondering why their heavy investments in CRM software systems, extensive scripting of their staff, and even general customer service skills training have not yielded the smart return on investment they expected.[24]

Figure 2. Levels of brand loyalty

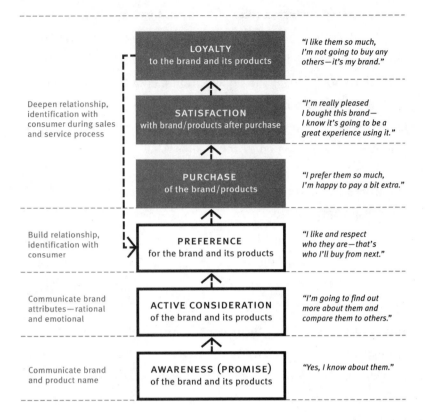

One hundred eighty-five major UK companies that spend a great deal of money on CRM technology were surveyed by Sistrum, CRM specialists that have been researching this technology since 1989. Sistrum found that, despite extensive CRM technology, only 8 percent of these 185 companies dealt effectively with something as simple as responding to urgent e-mail inquiries from potential customers.[25]

No doubt, customer and staff loyalty would dramatically improve if organizations instead spent only a small portion of what they annually invest in advertising or CRM systems on cohesively branding their internal cultures and educating their staff on how to deliver branded customer service. The impact of investing in staff training on the bottom line has been demonstrated multiple times. The American Society for Training and Development (ASTD), for example, compared the economic performance of companies that spend at the high end on employee training with those companies that do not invest in their staff. It found that for high investors in employee training,

- shareholder "market to book" value was 20 percent higher
- net sales per employee were 57 percent greater
- gross profits per employee were 37 percent steeper[26]

There are bright glimpses of brand-building service, including Nordstrom, Disney, Southwest Airlines, Pret a Manger, and Vodafone. Yet even the good organizations that have worked on branding their customer service do not always deliver. One of our Australian TMI colleagues, Tony Aveling, was in a Disneyland store, shopping for memories to take home with him in what he thought was an "amazing wonderland." He told the clerk helping him, "It must be fabulous working at a place like this." This representative of Disneyland (whether a direct employee or not) looked at him and said, "I hate it"—maybe the truth but remarkably off-brand.

The limitations of generic customer skills training

While few managers who purchase customer service programs for their staff think they are buying generic customer service skills training programs, in fact, that is what many do. Most customer service training companies have service programs (delivered on tape, on CD, or in person) that they offer to a wide range of high-end and low-end companies across a variety of industries. They sell the same program to multiple companies based on the idea that the same style of service delivery is going to create loyalty to an infinite range of different brands.

The public has leaped ahead of organizations in this area. Consumers do not hold one idea of service in their minds; the public is not generic when it comes to service. When evaluating customer service, consumers hold a multitude of personal, specific, and unique expectations about services and products relating to specific brands. Customers have different service expectations for banks than they do for retail shops. They also view one retail store differently from another. Sam's Club or Costco is not viewed the same as Nordstrom or Saks Fifth Avenue. With generic service, the experience customers ultimately have inside Costco compared to Saks Fifth Avenue could be the same, but customers walk into the two stores and shop with totally different expectations.

on-brand

We have noticed at Costco that the clerks look at products customers purchase as they pass through the checkout lines. The clerks sometimes ask where the customer found the product in the store. With their curiosity, they subtly emphasize how merchandise rapidly changes at Costco. The clerks also comment on the great price of certain products—not the staple items, such as peanut butter, but the unusual higher end items. It reinforces part of the unspoken Costco brand message: "We've got such great values that you need to buy them now. If you don't, the merchandise probably will not be there when you return."

It is difficult to distinguish your brand position from another organization's brand when offering advertising that looks like everyone else's. In the same way, generic service will not enhance your customer's experience about the uniqueness of your brand. Customer exchanges must illuminate features of the brand promise or brand values, such as in the above Costco example.

Generic service in the airline industry

Bland, undistinguished service and airplanes that all look alike is how the airline business, by and large, has turned itself into a commodity. Very few airlines are successful in distinguishing the brand of their service. It has not always been this way. Pacific Southwest Airlines (PSA), starting in California in 1949 and operating until 1986 when it was purchased by US Airways, had a unique look and feel to it. It was the fun airline.[27] PSA passengers had fun flying; employees had fun working.

Other airlines had a formal look, decked out with blue uniforms, expressing the business of serious flying. PSA stewardesses, as they were called at that time, donned shocking pink, fuchsia, and orange uniforms cut high on the leg (noted for their attractiveness, they wore hot pants under their miniskirts in case their skirts hiked up while they were putting items in the overhead bins, which many passengers waited to happen!), with jauntily perched tams on their heads, and shod in orange go-go boots. They were once referred to as "Cupcakes in the Sky." Employees got married in the air on PSA.[28] They were always called by their first names. The sense of a PSA family was carefully nurtured. They did not see themselves as employed by PSA; rather they saw themselves as PSA. To this day, almost twenty years later, they gather annually in San Diego to swap stories.

Their philosophy placed emphasis on innovation. Service was pushed by senior management and implemented by employees. Passengers were pampered with themed flights. Lost baggage claims were vigorously and promptly handled! This is the antithesis of generic airline service.

Former passengers were so enamored of PSA that today they still buy T-shirts commemorating the airline. The smile painted on the front of the aircraft said it all. PSA's slogan was "The world's friendliest airline," and the staff delivered. People had a good time flying on the California airline.

After the purchase by US Airways and the merger was sealed, US Airways did a major housecleaning, throwing away those outrageous PSA uniforms and getting rid of most of the senior staff. Former PSA employees still mourn the loss of their airline. The deal was closed the day after American Airlines bought a chief PSA competitor, another unique airline, Air California. Air California became homogenized into American Airlines, and California lost both its smiling, distinctive, and fun-filled airlines.

on-brand

Here is what a former Air Cal flight attendant says about that time period. "I was a stewardess with Air Cal from 1967 to 1973, and it was one of the best times of my life! I think what made it unique was the fact they hired married women, some with children. I had a four-year-old daughter when I was hired and Air Cal made sure you were taking care of your child and were able to work too. It was like family, very small and everyone cared about you and your family. I believe I was the no. 8 stew hired, so you can see how small it was! Our training, other than the safety training, was to make the passengers our no. 1 priority, and we did. I don' t think there will ever be another Air Cal; it was the best and most people-oriented airline I have ever seen."[29]

Most airlines today have not distinguished themselves with their physical products, and, with rare exception, they certainly have not done it with their service. Listen to the flying public and they will tell you most airlines are remarkably alike. The big differentiators for most airlines are routes, advertising, and fares.

It is possible to offer a commodity product, such as coffee, and then create such a unique brand position that the average consumer visits a location eighteen times a month—as Starbucks has done.[30] But you cannot wrap that coffee service in generic packaging or experiences and expect to stand out from the local diner. And you miss a real opportunity to distinguish your brand if your staff offers generic service, albeit good generic service. From a business perspective, you miss the opportunity to elicit the feeling in consumers that they absolutely must return to Starbucks despite long lines and coffee twice as expensive as that of its competitors.

Why scripting won't work with branded customer service

Some organizations work hard at grounding their brand in their culture, but the vast majority are not systematic about this. Most marketing departments assume that culture work has been completed once a marketing agency has shaped their brand, or they never consider creating a service culture their responsibility in the first place. In addition, all too many organizations don't know how to live and deliver their brands without tightly scripting service staff, which makes them seem constrained and unnatural.

Nido Qubein, chairman of Great Harvest Bread, relates the experience of talking on a toll-free line with a major telecommunications company. At the end of the conversation, the woman he had been talking with said, "Thank you for calling ____." Nido knows that this particular company has spent huge sums of money to get staff to have the last word at the end of every telephone conversation with a "thank you" to the customer.

So Nido, in an experimental mood, responded, "No. Thank *you* for helping me by providing such wonderful service." There was a slight hesitation at the other end of the phone line. The woman must have figured out that if she hung up the phone at that moment, she would not have had the last "thank you" that she was explicitly told to provide. And she was likely being taped!

"No, really sir, I must thank you," she responded. When Nido tells this story, he indicates that he was in an airport and had thirty minutes to kill before his plane boarded. So he said, "No, no, no. It is I who must thank you." This exchange went on a few more times, at which point the woman exclaimed, "No, darn it, *thank you.*" And cut off the call.

When supervisors write scripts for their customer service representatives, they are effectively telling the customers that they know exactly what needs to be said to deliver good service. First, we don't believe they can possibly know about every situation and every customer to make word-scripting work in all situations. Second, in so doing, they limit the staff's scope to connect with customers in an authentic manner. Scripting turns service encounters into simple transactions and does not benefit from the transformational impact that is possible when a brand touches at a heart and head level.

Unfortunately, scripted approaches to customer service are common as organizations attempt to measure against standards. Admittedly, scripts are easier to measure than free-flowing conversations, which is no doubt their inherent appeal. But tightly defined, compliance-driven scripting speaks to a remarkable lack of confidence in frontline staff to deliver appropriate and branded service on their own.

If service providers are given the freedom to express the brand that they support, then customers will have the sense that they are being treated as people and not as customers. If this does not happen, we agree with Professor Douglas Holt at Harvard University, who argues that customers will become even more cynical than they are if every customer touch point is experienced as a blatant promotion for the brand. This is definitely not what branded customer service is about![31]

Part of the difficulty is that many organizations have gotten too tightly caught up in measuring quality standards a la the founder of the quality movement, W. Edwards Deming.[32] Many believe that if we define and measure service delivery precisely enough (just as we do with product assembly), then somehow good service will have been delivered. Yet it is the outcome of the experience, evaluated from the customers' perspective about what they have been led to believe should happen, that is the true measuring stick.

As one of our colleagues, Anne Bogelund-Jensen of TMI, Denmark, likes to say, "You can't standardize your service, but you can set standards for your service." Once a service brand has been defined, that definition is basically static until human interaction makes it dynamic.

Our Lucaya brand study: a case of inspired on-brand behaviors

Hutchinson Whampoa, a major international trading company, through a series of complicated negotiations acquired ownership of a rundown property in the Bahamas. It took on the Herculean task of converting one hotel, building two others, and combining them into a first-class unified major resort, complete with a casino. Since Grand Bahama Island was not a tourist destination, the challenge was considerable.

Hutchinson started off right. It brought in one of the best UK brand imaging companies, Wolff Olins, which had worked with Hutchinson on a previous brand initiative, Orange Telecom, a UK telecommunication company. The Orange Telecom campaign set records in the telecom industry. In a remarkably short time it became a billion-dollar brand and today is one of the top one hundred brands in the world.

The hotel division of Hutchinson understood that it needed to capture the passion of its staff in order to succeed. Wolff Olins wrapped the Our Lucaya brand proposition around the unique people on Grand Bahama Island, known for their friendliness and desire to share. The decision was made to highlight the culture of the legendary Lucaya Indians, renowned for their hospitality. The brand idea was to create an "experience of participation" sharing with the distinctive Grand Bahamians.

Our Lucaya's brand induction program

In working with this client, our challenge was to take the defined brand promise and values developed by Wolff Olins and shape them into a communication experience that the local Bahamian population would embrace and deliver. The current attitudes on the property were first assessed. After a deep immersion in the Bahamian culture, we were able to pinpoint the challenges inherent in a situation where local Bahamians were being managed predominantly by professional European hoteliers and dealing with American and European guests. The high standards of the Europeans had to be met while the Bahamians needed inspiration to take ownership of the brand.

The developed brand communication experiences became a brand statement. By the time these brand induction programs had touched fifteen hundred Our Lucaya staff members, the passion for the "ourness" of Our Lucaya was firmly embraced by the Bahamians.

Our Lucaya's brand proposition stands for six ideas: vibrancy, engaging, energizing, personal, worth remembering, and refreshing. Since everyone had different interpretations of these words, staff were asked to define what these words meant to them. Staff created posters and then danced, sang, or otherwise explained the significance of each of the words. Huge amounts of energy were released and right away staff knew that they were connected to something different than just a hotel job. The posters were hung on walls around the resort, and contests were organized to select the best posters. Wolff Olins had selected striking and evocative pictures to go with each of the six brand ideas that were also used in the Our Lucaya advertising campaign. These widely displayed pictures and posters helped to inspire and reinforce staff ideas about what they needed to do.

In order to be engaging in a manner that fit a resort environment, staff were taught how to ask open-ended questions of the guests. This was a skill set that required considerable coaching because hotel staff around the world tend to ask questions that can easily be answered by a single yes or no or other one-word answer ("Is this your first visit here? Did you fly in?"), which is not very engaging. Instead they were taught possibilities such as, "What special things did you do today?"

To demonstrate "personal," housekeepers were told that who they were as individuals (personal) was desirable and on-brand for guests to see. When set free to be themselves at work, they dressed up their vacuum cleaners as people and gave them names. Vibrant language also was modeled and practiced. The golf course was never described as "up to standard." It became "a green paradise on earth" or "a breath of fresh air in the morning." Most of the expressive Bahamian staff immediately embraced this practice as it so directly mirrors their culture.

Giving the Bahamians permission
to fly like swirling flocks of birds

Once the Bahamians understood what was expected of them, they allowed the enormous joy and creativity in their vibrant language to be shared with the guests. They were encouraged to use their distinctive local patois, which involves repeating words. Bahamians do not say, "Good morning," to each other. They say, "Morn, morn." The key message of the program printed in the staff Brand Book was "We want people to go away from Our Lucaya feeling the service they received was not only top-notch but refreshingly different in its style and approach." It was up to the staff to deliver this different service.

In the publicity that followed, Peta Peter, TMI's program director for this project, was quoted as saying, "We looked at what it is about Grand Bahama Island that is unique, and it came back to how they treat a guest. It's like, 'My house is your house.'"[33] Peta coached staff to explore feelings of self-worth, styles of communication, and strategies to handle difficult internal situations—not the most typical of topics in a customer service program. While ideas for communication were suggested, staff were never once told what they had to do in a precise manner.

In multiple reinforcing ways, however, staff were told over and over again that all they had to do was be their natural Bahamian selves and they would be brand distinctive: vibrant, personal, worth remembering, engaging, energizing, and refreshing. If they delivered their Bahamian culture with a high level of service standards, the reputation for Our Lucaya would spread.

James McDougall, director of training for Our Lucaya, summarized the process, "The main goal was to get everyone to buy into the 'all a we is one family' concept—the local Bahamian expression for the whole family pulling together to clean and get the house ready before the relatives or special guests arrive."[34] Generic customer service might have created good customer service delivery, but the spirit and brand promise of Our Lucaya would have been present only in the resort's advertising. Only a specific branded service delivery would work.

3

Road Map to
Branded Customer Service

Even though empirical evidence tells us that developed brands correlate positively with financial performance, the power of branding is remarkably still largely unrecognized by many businesspeople as it applies to their own organizations.[1] When we speak on this topic, we often ask how many in our audience can state exactly what their brand promise is or what their brand values are. We even offer prizes to those who can. Very few people have this information on the tips of their tongues, and we frequently cart our prizes home with us.

Research by brand experts Scott Davis and Michael Dunn that included ninety global corporations shows that 45 percent of managers lack an understanding of the positioning of their own brand.[2] Sixty-two percent of Davis and Dunn's survey respondents described a lack of senior management support for their brands. Both of these deficiencies were judged by the corporations as threats to their long-term business success.

If this lack of brand knowledge and support is representative of management, it is reasonable to conclude that the pattern is even truer for customer service representatives. Yet Prophet's (the San Francisco brand consulting firm) 2002 Best Practices Study concluded that "despite an overwhelming belief in the impact of personal contact [on brands] . . . only 41 percent of managers considered investment in customer service an important part of their brand-building efforts."[3]

Linking human behavior, policies, and systems with branding clearly presents both practical and conceptual challenges that have not yet been entirely addressed by even the most successful brands. But we know that the signposts on the road to enhancing brand ideas with customer service minimally include

- teaching everyone how your marketing, advertising, mission statement, and so on define your brand and how this definition impacts the type of service required to reinforce the brand
- getting everyone—management and all employees—to understand and embrace the elements of your branded customer service without scripting everyone
- inspiring all staff from the CEO to administrative staff, the sales team, and the shop clerk to deliver—and act out—the brand and its values on a *consistent basis*

Brand space: staff cannot deliver what they do not know

Many customer-facing employees do not have a brand service lens to evaluate their service delivery beyond good or bad generic service. They do not know the unique components of their brand, the brand's DNA. This is probably why so many service representatives are convinced they normally deliver good customer service. Viewed through a generic service lens, service was good if it was speedy, polite, and perhaps even friendly. However, these qualities do not necessarily deliver a specific brand experience.

Common sense tells us that in order to deliver branded service experiences, staff at a minimum must know

- the brand has value and means something specific

- everything an organization does potentially affects the brand—positively or negatively
- which specific behaviors reinforce the brand

Once staff understand the DNA of their brand (see chapter 4), we encourage them to use the terms "on-brand" and "off-brand" to identify behaviors that are aligned with the brand and those that are not. This will help everyone easily understand the role of customer service in relationship to the brand. The concept of on-brand and off-brand encourages quick evaluation of service interactions on the criteria that matter the most. We have found these terms are extremely easy to use, are rapidly adopted by employees, and provide everyone with powerful verbal tools.

Four customer service strategies: which one is for you?

Customer service strategies cover the gamut from seeing customers as a necessary evil to the concept on which this book is based, branded customer service. Summarized in table 1 are four strategic customer service options.

Why is it that more companies don't implement a complete branded service strategy? Lack of awareness is certainly a factor for many. However, part of the explanation is that creating an environment where on-brand service is offered to customers requires managers to authentically value and respect their service providers. Frankly, this respect isn't always present. A branded approach toward service must also acknowledge and value the dynamic, human exchange that is the essence of an interaction between customers and service providers. They would like to believe that their service strategy is at least at a competitive level. But their implementation in terms of how they treat their own staff is at a "cost" level. They fool themselves. But the public isn't fooled.

Another reason more companies do not implement a branded service strategy is that many service providers see their interaction with customers as a battle. If you listen to people within organizations talk about their customers, you hear name-calling, see rule implementation that demonstrates a lack of trust, or experience the fear many companies have precisely because they know customers are a necessity. As a result, they don't fully implement strategies based on creating cooperation between customers and staff by delivering what has been promised. They don't understand that this is the most direct way to win trust, support, and loyalty.

But probably the most realistic answer for many is that the phone keeps ringing and people get distracted. They are simply too busy handling day-to-day operational requirements of their business to engage in a branded service strategy that requires time and attention. Branding your customer service starts with a conscious decision to pursue this service strategy, and then it requires ongoing attention. It isn't done accidentally.

How to polish your service lens to reflect your brand promises

To be branded, customer service must possess four attributes.

1. *It must be unique.* The service exchange must have some minimal components that are different from other service exchanges. After all, if brands are unique, then so must be the service that reflects that particular brand. This uniqueness can be attained in the way that brand characteristics are combined or emphasized.

   For example, friendly and secure service is different from friendly and exciting service. And a brand that emphasizes excitement and at the same time is friendly is differentiated from one that prioritizes friendliness with a dash of excitement thrown in. Given the vast number of possibilities to touch customers logically and emotionally, it is relatively easy to carve out a distinct space for your uniquely branded service. "It absolutely, positively, has to be there

Table 1. Customer service strategies

STRATEGY	SERVICE	ORGANIZATIONAL BEHAVIOR	TARGETED OUTCOMES	LIKELY RESULTS
CUSTOMER SERVICE AS A COST	*Seen as not necessary, extraneous* *Seen as a short-term transaction*	**Policy:** *Don't trust either customers or staff* **Rules:** *Make no exceptions* **Approach:** *Take care of the organization first, customers second* **Training:** *Extremely limited; technical or product training when necessary* **Management:** *Short-term focus; quick fixes for all problems*	*Highest possible margins for each transaction*	*Customers buy on price and availability* *Staff stay based on salary levels* *Engagement with company is very low* *Organization operates as a commodity*
CUSTOMER SERVICE AS A NECESSITY	*Required because competitors are offering it* *Seen as a cost, rather than a marketing investment*	**Policy:** *Be nice to customers* **Rules:** *Limited empowerment of staff* **Approach:** *Do what is necessary to keep the customers but no more* **Training:** *Generic customer training for frontline staff; "smile training"* **Management:** *Short-term focus; reaction about customer problems*	*Avoid noticeable customer dissatisfaction* *Satisfied but not loyal customers* *Aim for zero filing of complaints*	*Fewer lost customers* *Repeat business based on prices, availability, and customer inertia* *Engagement with company is low* *Organization operates as a commodity*

CUSTOMER SERVICE AS A COMPETITIVE ADVANTAGE	Seen as a strategic measure to develop business	**Policy:** Exceed customer expectations **Rules:** Staff empowered to take care of customers **Approach:** Delight, knock socks off, create raving fans, customers for a lifetime **Training:** Packaged training with titles similar to the ones above **Management:** Longer-term focus; direct involvement with customer service issues	Delighted customers High customer survey scores Bonuses awarded based on survey scores	Enhanced reputation for service Staff more likely to stay High levels of repeat business if product is solid Engagement with company is positive
CUSTOMER SERVICE AS AN ESSENTIAL LIVING EXPRESSION OF THE BRAND	Seen as a vital aspect of the organization Seen as the brand in action	**Policy:** Every touch point reflects the brand **Rules:** Brand promise reflected in internal policies and procedures **Approach:** Service delivery that is on-brand **Training:** Tailored brand education for everyone **Management:** Long-term focus; management involved in every phase of on-brand service	Brand is integrated into total organizational culture Aim for reinforcement of brand messages among customers and staff	High percentage of engaged customers who become brand advocates Engaged and empowered staff; feel like they own the brand Customers feel emotional connection to company Increased brand equity; higher profits

overnight" is different from "a reasonably priced alternative" to sending your packages.

2. *It must amplify or deliver the core brand promise.* Branded service must be expressed through behaviors that demonstrate the core brand promise. At Disney hotels, for example, housekeepers take stuffed animals left behind by children staying in the rooms they attend to and arrange them in an inviting position. When the young owners return to their rooms after a long day at Disneyland, they are welcomed by the open arms of their beloved toys. Simultaneously clean rooms, family entertainment, and the core Disney brand are all delivered at once!

3. *It must be delivered with awareness.* Delivering good generic service can be so natural that service providers do not have to think much about it. They know their jobs, and many are instinctively friendly and quick. But branded service, especially when it is noteworthy, normally requires a decision on the part of staff to do something or not. This is why creating an environment that supports living the brand within the organization makes it more likely that staff will remember to deliver the brand in their behavior.

   This is also why it is not possible to just tell your staff to go out and deliver a particular style of branded customer service. People are not innately knowledgeable about how to do that. Staff must not only fully understand the brand, but they must also explore how their service can represent the brand in action. In addition to being brand savvy, they must have the required skills, systems, resources, and tools to help them deliver the brand.

4. *It must be delivered within a defined and consistent range.* If service is not consistent, customers will assume that the experience was specific to the individual with whom they interacted. They will not see the service as representative of the brand.[4] Even the worst service organizations have a few outstanding people. And some have

service providers who are so off-brand with their skills that they can give the entire organization a black eye.

off-brand

Travelocity, the Internet travel provider, has a very good reputation, is very successful, and has worked hard to distinguish itself. But even the best in the field can fail at always being on-brand. The following e-mail is duplicated as it was received from a reputedly well-trained Travelocity service representative, complete with at least nine glaring errors that have been underscored. Since over 50 percent of online customers seek help when they make travel arrangements, a single e-mail can send a message that the entire organization doesn't value precision or accuracy, both of which are critical in the travel industry.

When you are ready to book a flight you have the option to have it Round-trip or one way. Just choose. To find the lowest fare, you can use our new Best Fare Finder. With this option on the Book a Flight page, you can entr your city pair, and the number of travelers and Travelocity wil find the lowest fare. YOu do not have to enter dates for this option, ti will give you a comploete list of the dates the desried fare isavailable and let you choose. If you have specific dates that you would liketo travel, you can use or 9 Best option. With this option, Travelocity finds the best itineraries based on the dates of travel.

Please let us know if you need further assistance.

Have a nice day!
Regards,
Elizabeth
Travelocity.com

Two types of branded customer service

Making a strategic decision to implement customer service as your brand in action makes most sense if your organization provides service to support products or if service is basically what consumers buy from you. If this is your business model, your service can reinforce your brand, your service can be your brand, or your service can be a combination of these two.

Service can be offered in a way that reinforces your product brand

Manufacturing companies that offer products requiring add-on service are strongly defined by their products. In these instances, using service experiences to reinforce the product brand makes sense, such as with BMW and Mercedes.

Our Lucaya, the resort complex discussed in the previous chapter, is a good example of a remarkable physical product that is but one part of its total customer offering. Personal service shares equal billing with the glorious resort setting. The branding company that worked with Our Lucaya developed a series of brand attributes that show up in all of the resort's physical touch points including advertising, the resort's design, and offerings such as room decor, restaurant themes, and recreational activities. Once the brand was strategized, the staff were offered training in how to deliver the Our Lucaya brand identity at the touch point of human interaction.

Service can be branded so it is the dominant aspect of the brand

Organizations that offer their staff's competency or behavior (consulting firms, accountancies, medical care, food services, entertainment, etc.) can make their service their brand.[5] When implementing this approach, the service brand needs to be defined in the same way that a product brand is defined: that is, the brand promises, brand values, personality, and so on. Businesses whose products are essentially commodities or ones with built-in deficits can also effectively use this approach.

Southwest Airlines is a good example of this type of branded customer service. Southwest's service is branded as fun and high-spirited, which Southwest staff deliver magnificently. Southwest's style is noted for its comedic and caring personalized attention. Combined with low fares, reliable and clean airplanes, and the ability to stay on time, Southwest covers rather notable deficits in other material aspects of its service, most of which enable the low pricing and the on-time records. You cannot reserve a seat at Southwest, for example, resulting in long lines at the gates. If you don't arrive early, there is a good chance you will occupy a middle seat at the back of the plane. Southwest offers no interline luggage transfers, so if you switch airlines on your trip, you have to transfer your own luggage. There is no first class. No meals are served; peanuts and pretzels are the best you will consume. And some seats are uncomfortably configured so you sit facing other passengers. This enables Southwest to carry six more passengers on such planes. Southwest makes no apologies for the decisions it has made about the quality of this aspect of its service.

Southwest has turned a commodity product (mass transportation) into a desired and successful brand through a consistent and pleasant delivery. We recently overheard two passengers discussing Southwest while flying on United. Both agreed they hated the no-assigned-seating approach of Southwest, but they entertained each other repeating magnificently funny lines delivered by Southwest flight attendants.

Southwest's leaders understand that their brand values can be delivered only by encouraging all their staff to make positive emotional connections with customers. On a recent flight that Paul took from Los Angeles to Las Vegas, he was first amused with the cabin announcement that greeted the passengers: "Buckle up, folks. We're off to lost wages." The authenticity of the cabin crew's interactions with individual customers was even more impressive. As a weary business traveler, Paul was treated quite differently from three young men opposite him weekending in Sin City. On-brand service was delivered in both cases, even though the needs around Southwest's brand values of "fun" and "love" were very different.

Southwest staff are told to be real and authentic, express their individuality, make good judgments, and apply common sense when situations do not fit a defined category. Flight crews frequently do this in a self-disparaging way that says to passengers, "Our secret is that we're all in this thing (uncomfortable air travel) together." It's very appealing.

Customers feel well taken care of because Southwest is extremely clear as to what it is delivering: reliability, low prices, and high-spirited, fun customer service. Southwest began with the idea of creating low-cost airfares for people who could not normally afford to fly. Southwest's branded service has been so successful that it has extended its patronage way beyond that market. It now carries more passengers than any other airline in the United States.[6] Southwest not only is the world's most profitable airline, it also shares its wealth in a staff profit-sharing plan that is remarkably generous. For all these reasons, the airline is regularly listed as one of the best places to work.

Vodafone New Zealand, like many telecommunication companies today, believes that it can no longer maintain its competitive edge solely through product advances. The timeline on duplication of its mobile cell products by competitors shrank from two years to two months within the space of five years. Vodafone management has concluded that the only way it can create a sustainable point of differentiation is through a defined service experience. Since implementing this strategy, its market share has risen from 19 percent to 52 percent, which Vodafone largely attributes to its investment in service branding.

Nordstrom provides another such example. Basically, all department stores have access to the same goods, so defining the customers that the store wants to attract through product choice is critical. Nordstrom has made a name for itself by focusing on service delivery for upscale shoppers.

Nordstrom staff have also perfected the art of offering "every once in a while" outrageous service experiences that bind their customers to them. Their service delivery at times is so unusual that they are frequently written about in customer service books. There is an ongoing buzz in the marketplace about Nordstrom; an informal group of loyal shoppers even calls its members Nordies. As a result of its unusual delivery of service—every once in a while—and its famous no-hassles exchange policy, Nordstrom generally sells its merchandise at full price, getting by with a minimal number of sales to attract crowds. Nor is it forced to engage in as much advertising as Macy's.

on-brand

Las Vegas radio station Lite 100.5's breakfast announcer, Melanie, relayed a "wow" brand story right before Mother's Day. Melanie had delayed getting her mother a gift, so she called a Nordstrom store in the city where her mother lives and requested that a selected gift be sent. She then lamented that it was too late to have it arrive before Mother's Day. "No problem," said the clerk. "I live close by your mother. I'll drop it off on my way home." Melanie said, "I'm not shopping anyplace else, ever again," as heard all over Las Vegas.

On its Web site, Nordstrom states its brand promise: "We remain committed to the simple idea our company was founded on, earning the trust of our customers, one at a time."

Albertsons, the grocery store, offers yet another such example. Again, a grocery store is basically a commodity business, but Albertsons has created a strong brand through the service it provides to shoppers. This includes its material service, such as well-lighted, very clean stores and well-laid-out, well-stocked shelves. The stores have great hours. In addition, staff are friendly, they walk you to goods when you ask where something is located, they emphasize how much you saved by shopping with them, and they are also conscious about relieving the pressure of long queues at the checkout. Their brand differentiators are ease of shopping, best promotional offerings, freshness in produce and baked goods, health-care accessibility with a pharmacy, and the best consumer selections. Many of these differentiators are delivered behind the scenes, which is part of Albertsons' service success. And it shows in its customer service scores. The Albertsons in Summerlin, Las Vegas, recently conducted a customer survey and received the highest scores possible—from 100 percent of the customers surveyed! That's unheard of in the survey business.

Berrett-Koehler (BK), the publisher of this book, is also a good example of a developed service brand. While not as well known a name as Random House or Simon and Schuster, for those who know BK, it has a strong reputation as a publisher that lives the values of the books it publishes. Its books share a common theme: offering businesses competitive advantages while making them better places at which to work. BK's service brand is "walking the talk," intense attention, and partnership with authors. Its staff read all its published books, it lavishes personal attention on authors (through its unique author's day), and it encourages authors to have a voice in a variety of publishing decisions frequently denied by other publishers.

The deficits that Berrett-Koehler covers with this type of service and authentic personal relationships are not paying book advances;

paying royalties only once a year (and they aren't the highest in the industry); having placements in bookstores that are not as extensive as, say, Random House's; and expecting that authors will be fully involved with marketing their own books. While not all authors like to work this way, big-name authors, nonetheless, line up to work with BK. The buzz among authors who are looking for a publisher is that an agreement with BK is a plum contract and a unique experience in the publishing world.

Berrett-Koehler is a striking example because it also demonstrates how branded customer service can act as an equalizer in the battle for brand recognition. For companies that do not have the resources or the appetite to advertise and market extensively, it is the means by which they can build their brand over time.

Pret a Manger, a UK fast-food sandwich shop, is another strong example of a company that has been able to create an enviable brand within its market segment with no advertising. Pret a Manger's chief executive, Andrew Rolfe, emphasizes that Pret's brand and its business are indistinguishable:

> The minute you try and separate the brand from the business it becomes artificial. We're not concerned about having consistency of brand so much as about consistency of purpose that flows throughout the whole of the organization. It doesn't actually matter what we write on the napkins or say through advertising, all that matters is that when you go into a Pret shop you get that set of experiences that describes Pret.[7]

The message on Pret's bags is this: "We are passionate about food. We go to great lengths to ensure that the food we sell is fresh, healthy and of the highest quality. Please call about anything to do with our shops, our food or our hardworking wonderful people. The good, the bad and the ugly."

The last time we visited one of its shops and ate incredibly delicious and fresh sandwiches, we asked its "wonderful people," "What's it like to work here?" The response was a happy giggle, a big smile, and "It's great! We love it"—brand delivered.

Branding with bad service: it can be done

Some businesses have used their service to brand themselves in an unusual way. That is, they have turned bad service into an art form so that it, in effect, becomes a crucial part of the brand experience. Several restaurants employ this type of bad service branding. One restaurant in Dallas, Texas, features waitresses who noisily chew gum and shout at customers. It's a show, and they obviously have fun delivering it.

Some high-end boutique shops practice snooty behavior toward their customers to demonstrate their exclusivity. Clerks will address you as "my dear" in a condescending tone of voice with a fake British accent, while looking down their noses at you. It makes a certain group of shoppers feel good about paying higher prices—especially if they see the clerks treating other customers this way.

Simon Cowell, one of the *American Idol* television show judges, has branded himself as a controversial critic. He keeps getting invited back to judge; people find him clever, and they enjoy groaning when he makes his brutally frank and negative comments. He helps keep loyal fans watching *American Idol. Queer Eye for the Straight Guy,* the big Bravo television hit, is branding itself to a large degree with cynical remarks about unkempt straight men.

This type of negative branding is unusual, but when it works, it can be a draw for a specific market segment. The limitation is that once you become recognized and applauded for this type of delivery, it is very difficult to shift to another style without losing your devoted customer base.

on-brand

Two UK star chefs, Gordon Ramsay and Raymond Blanc, prepare extraordinary food in their kitchens. They have each been awarded a number of Michelin stars. But their personalities may be as much a draw as their recipes. Gordon Ramsay engages in a coarse dialogue with both staff and customers. Raymond Blanc charms them. They are described as "chefs with attitude."

People must book reservations at their restaurants months in advance, and the two chefs' different personalities reinforce their distinctiveness and passion about food. Both chefs magnify their unique brand through their differentiated behavior, passion, and attitudes that make their culinary skills in the kitchen all the more attractive.[8]

Impact of branding your customer service

Four significant benefits can be accrued from branding your service experiences.

1. *Branding customer service returns control of the definition of good service to the organization.* When companies offer generic service that is not designed to reinforce their brands, customers judge the received service based on their personally held standards of good and bad service. This makes it difficult for organizations to define good and bad service in their own terms. Under these circumstances, staff will not know exactly when they have delivered good or bad service until the customer tells them. If you go into a Costco store, you will find it difficult to locate employees who can tell you where items are. It's expected and partially enables the store's discount pricing, so the absence of an adequate number of employees

walking the floor is not considered bad service. However, if you went into a retail shop that was promoted as a personalized shopping experience, you would experience the unavailability of sales clerks as bad service.

Just as manufacturing companies set their own standards for quality, so, too, should service companies set their own service standards. Let the public know what to expect, and then get your staff to meet this defined service standard in the same way a line supervisor checks for product quality to a certain standard.

Southwest Airlines has been known to send customers who complain about its practice of not assigning seats a letter that, in effect, reads, "Thank you for having been a customer of ours. We will miss you." Southwest is not about to move away from its brand promise (low fares and reliability) by changing systems that make possible a turnaround of aircraft in twenty minutes.

Consumers know that a commercial interest is present in every transaction, and they can become quite cynical when employees present themselves as working exclusively for the consumers' benefit. No doubt, most people would just as soon staff be up-front about this. When they know how the brand has been defined and that there are no apologies for that, the customer-supplier relationship becomes more authentic. We were told once by Southwest, "We don't offer interline transfers of luggage so we can remain profitable. Our competitors aren't." While not meeting our wishes, such a statement is nonetheless honest and refreshing to hear.

2. *Branded service lets the organization set standards for the five dimensions of service in relationship to its brand.* The five classic dimensions of customer service (ServQual, as they are called) are based on extensive consumer research. They were identified at Texas A&M in the 1960s and include reliability, assuredness, tangibility, empathy, and responsiveness. (A further explanation and application

follow in chapter 4.) When service is branded, an organization can write specific brand standards for each of these five classic dimensions of service.

3. *Branded customer service is a strong equalizer for brands.* By consistently delivering its brand promise, an organization can develop a strong brand without a huge advertising budget. U.S.-based Krispy Kreme Doughnuts exemplifies how brands can develop significant market share without spending a penny on media advertising. Krispy Kreme has become known in the marketplace by occupying a clearly defined brand space and making sure that customer experiences match the brand. Because of its remarkable rarity, there are a lot of public relations possibilities when an organization delivers its brand promise.

4. *Successful branding can create quasi monopolies.* It may be extremely difficult to topple Coca-Cola from its number one position on Interbrand's annual list of the top one hundred brands worldwide—or even to get on the list. But branded customer service can make it possible for small brands with limited marketing budgets to be tops in their local markets.

A product or service whose delivery reinforces brand promises can become a magnet within the target population the brand wishes to attract. Starbucks, for example, is not the number one coffeehouse brand in every market. And sometimes an obscure brand can capture public attention by standing out from big-name brands, such as is the case with a previously little-known restaurant in New York City. The Grocery was recently named by *Zagat Survey* as the seventh-best restaurant in Manhattan. It's an inexpensive place to eat, no liquor is served, and no one will be there to take your coat. What the Grocery has created is a reputation as a solid neighborhood restaurant, delivering the excellent food and service it promises at an appropriate rate. According to the owner, who was made a little nervous by the acclaim, "I don't want people to be disappointed, but we're not going to change the way we do things."[9]

Branded customer service and themed customer service

Pine and Gilmore's book, *The Experience Economy*, has led the charge on the importance of paying attention to customer experiences. The authors predict that the only sustainable businesses in the future will be those that offer a distinct, themed customer experience. To set the record straight, while branded service experiences are related to the type of themed customer experiences suggested in *The Experience Economy*, they are not identical.

Certainly all branded service creates experiences in the general sense of *experience*, meaning anything observed or lived through. But a branded service experience can be delivered in ways other than through themed customer experiences.

Not everyone wants a themed customer experience

In Las Vegas you can have your pick of themed customer environments and service offerings. The Disney parks are all themed experiences. However, not all consumers desire a constant array of themed experiences. For example, when you fill your car up with gasoline, do you want a themed experience, or do you just want a tank of gas—offered with solid customer service skills? To entice you back to a particular gasoline brand, it would be good if the service were also on-brand. But it does not necessarily need to be an elaborate, orchestrated experience for which you are willing to take extra time to enjoy and pay higher gasoline prices.

Some products and businesses are successfully based on commodity business models. And many companies offer brand promises without creating themed experiences. Costco is a solid example of a company that reinforces its brand in myriad ways. Its type of customer experience, however, is a far cry from that of Starbucks, which is viewed as one of the major customer retailers of themed experiences.

Branding your customer service does not mean you have to put on a show. You can, for example, answer the telephone in an on-brand manner without delivering a themed experience. Furthermore, if the business community confuses a well-designed on-brand banking experience, for example, with a Walt Disney–type entertainment experience, the result could place unreasonable demands on staff. For example, bank clubs could be easily overwhelmed if they had the responsibility to be precise about counting money and at the same time to entertain customers waiting in line. Nonetheless, both a branded nonthemed bank and a Walt Disney park need to offer consistent on-brand service—or their brands will suffer.

Build-A-Bear: successful themed experience

If you successfully build a themed service experience around the customers' shopping, there is no doubt that you can charge more. For example, people spend hours choosing the ingredients that will become their final one-of-a-kind bear in the popular Build-A-Bear stores (workshops, as they are called). The stores boast an average income of $700 per square foot compared to a retail average of $350. People buy add-ons from all the different stations they go through to enhance their basic $10 bear. It is a memorable experience to share with a child and certainly worth the extra money.

Build-A-Bear's branded service reflects its brand promise. You can read it on every page of the Build-A-Bear Web site and at every one of its stores: *personalization* (you build your own bear), *fun* (you watch your bear come to life and then get a birth certificate for it), *caring* (through a lost bear program), *connection* (through parties, news-letters), *hands-on* (you make the choices, touching all the while), and *memorable* (how could it not be?). These bears are so special they have registered names and seem almost alive. The initial target market of Build-A-Bear was girls up to twelve years old, but the experience has also attracted young boys and adults.

On-brand customer service deepens these emotional experiences through systems (for example, the lost bear program) that create staff-customer interactions supporting the Build-A-Bear brand. One such brand story is that of a young boy who came into a workshop to buy a replacement bear for the one he had lost. The boy chose a name that was very unusual for his new bear, and the clerk thought she had heard it before. She asked the boy if he had ever had another bear with the same name. When he answered yes, she searched for and found his lost bear, which had been returned to the store. Upon seeing the bear, the mother and boy broke into tears, and they went home with two bears.[10] The store had attempted to locate the boy earlier, but he had moved. This is "caring," one of the brand values brought to life and delivered with an exclamation point!

Build-A-Bear's themed service experience has to do with all the activities that children and adults can experience while in the store. It involves the stores' layout, their locations, their interactive hands-on process, and the product itself. There is a great deal of expense in making this experience happen. Build-A-Bear's branded service, which amplifies its brand proposition, is built on excellent generic service. Combined, they support the themed experience of building bears, and Build-A-Bear is the success it is today. The average customer returns five times per year—the workshops host memorable birthday parties. Even its Web page (http://www.buildabear.com) is an astonishing on-line experience. All of this adds up to revenues in excess of $160 million in 2002—in the teddy bear business![11]

When you just want a stuffed teddy bear and you have your lunch hour in which to purchase it, grabbing one off a shelf might be your best bet. Nonetheless, even while grabbing, you would still want a pleasant experience and courteous treatment. It would also be great for the reputation of the store if that service were on-brand.

Envelop You: successful (fictionalized) branded customer service

While we see these three service offerings (generic service, branded customer service, and themed customer experience) as related, they are also different from each other. We can best demonstrate this relationship by creating a fictionalized company.

We start an envelope and packaging materials company, a commodity business. To succeed, we have to manufacture envelopes and packaging material that meet our targeted market's needs. Regardless of how limited our customer interactions are (maybe we start out as a manufacturer and work through distributors and retailers), we still have to provide good supportive customer service (ServQual: reliability, assuredness, tangibility, empathy, and responsiveness) or our distributors will become tired of us. They will go someplace else to get their envelopes unless we have the cheapest prices.

We become so successful at our commodity business that we decide to differentiate our envelopes and packaging material by branding our products and service. We even open a few stores called Envelop You. Our brand proposition is "Packaging that envelops you with vintage, variety, and value." To enhance and deepen the knowledge of our brand, we communicate the brand through effective advertising, good product positioning, and clever public relations.

We have a lot of customer interaction with our direct customers, and we are careful to enhance the brand every time someone interacts with us. Our goal is to have people at least think of us when they have packaging needs. We want to become a household name. Our tagline is "If it's worth giving, it's worth enveloping." We have worked hard to get our staff to understand the uniqueness of the brand they represent. We not only offer training programs that emphasize excellent generic customer service skills, but we also pay particular attention to Envelop You brand service skills.

We have an on-brand internal culture. We have been very careful to make sure that the Envelop You brand concept is part of our human resources strategy, as for example in our employee benefits and recruitment. We know what "vintage, variety, and value" means at Envelop You. One unique strategy we use is to rotate people through all the positions in our shops, so no one gets bored.

Our staff know how to support our values because they live them every day in their work. To our customers they might say, "Oh, we have many choices that will work for you. And you'll be surprised at how little it costs." "Yes, this ribbon is of very high quality. In fact, many of our customers take this bow and put it at the top of their Christmas tree." And when customers pick up their packages, we serve them hot chocolate while they wait. We ask them if they would like our brand sticker, "Enveloped with Care by Envelop You," on their package. In addition, the staff do all of this with excellent generic customer skills; that is, they are reliable, assured, tangible, empathic, and responsive.

We get so good at this with our now dozens of Envelop You stores that we decide to create an innovative experience for our retail shops and online customers. We redesign our stores so they actually look like beautifully wrapped boxes. When people bring in something to be packaged, they get to watch the entire process accomplished with very fancy machines and highly trained package designers that we call Artistes. Customers choose every aspect of their packaging and walk out with pieces of enveloped art that they created. These packages are beautiful, we know for certain that some people keep the packaging intact and never look at the gift inside the box!

Part II

Embedding On-Brand Service into Your Organizational DNA

Part II begins by examining what is necessary to define the unique attributes of your brand, your brand DNA. We then consider a model called Inside-Out Branding, used by TMI when developing and analyzing customer service brand integration projects. This model sets the stage for the chapters on culture change, internal communications, brand champions, and human resources.

To succeed, your carefully developed brand promises must be integrated into multiple organizational support functions. Brand champions, those cheerleaders who can keep energy high for brand initiatives, are part of your capacity to make your brand resonate internally. Human resources, which we like to think of as the window to the corporate soul, may be the most important of these because of HR's far-ranging organizational impact. All of these aspects of internal communication affect your corporate culture.

We conclude part II with a case study of a multifaceted, sprawling U.S.-based corporation, The Isle of Capri Casinos, which provides a classic and important example of the effectiveness of senior management and an HR department working together to implement branded customer service.

4

Defining Your Brand DNA

Whether or not you have taken the time to formulate your brand, your organization, your service, and your products are still a brand. Your brand may not be on Interbrand's one hundred most valuable brands list; nonetheless, your brand is what consumers and staff think about you. Your choice is whether to take control of shaping your brand's destiny or to let consumers and your staff haphazardly define your brand. If customers define your brand, they will do so in large part based upon their experiences, influenced by employees who have no clear idea about the brand they represent.

What is your brand DNA

Defining brand DNA, the unique components of a brand, is key to beginning the process of consistently delivering on-brand service. This is a concept that most organizations struggle to understand, at least outside the marketing department. Many management teams have become conditioned to looking for the next quick fix solution that can be bolted onto their existing business infrastructures. While we were recently discussing branded customer service with a group of HR professionals and trainers, they simply said, "Show us the training program."

This mind-set is undoubtedly one of the major reasons so many service-related initiatives fail to deliver any real competitive edge.

Clayton Christensen and Michael Raynor highlighted this problem in their book, *The Innovators Solution*.[1] They use the analogy of man's early attempts in aviation, where researchers observed the correlation between birds, which have wings and feathers, and their ability to fly. Yet when man followed these apparent "best practices," the results were an unmitigated disaster.

If your requirement is to improve the level of generic skills, then a shrink-wrapped solution may suffice. But if it is about branding, about creating a point of true differentiation and distinctiveness, there is no one size that fits all. Branding is not something that you can copy from another company, no matter how successful it has been. We have heard many companies refer to their "internal brand," when all they mean is a stylized logo, color palette, and communication template developed for internal communications. Only by understanding the underlying processes that drive the relationship between brands and people can companies achieve successful alignment to customer service.

The underlying process of defining the space your brand occupies involves

- establishing a justification for the value of the brand and a picture of the brand's future aspirations
- defining how the brand's promises and differentiators are to be delivered
- clarifying how the brand is to be seen in the marketplace and establishing its personality in relationship to the organization's business ideas, staff capabilities, and customer needs

Figure 3, while not exhaustive, shows critical components that should be considered.

Figure 3. The DNA components of brand space

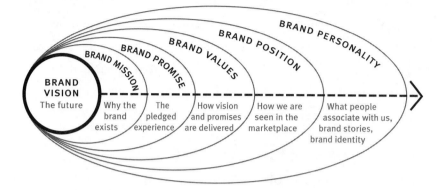

Brand professionals look at these components from a marketing perspective. Those who are interested in branding their customer service must look at each component as it relates to service delivery.

In defining brand DNA most comprehensively, brand strategists will undertake extensive research of various customer groups segmented by both demographic and psychological needs. They will peel back the layers in search of the underlying motivations and drivers of these groups. They will test the various competitor offerings to better understand what is working for consumers and what is not. Ideally, they will also analyze the internal culture to define what its unique characteristics are, what makes it special. Finally, they will analyze where the industry is heading in terms of its product and service offerings. All this will then be distilled to determine a core brand proposition supported by underlying brand values. Done well, this brand architecture will provide the basis for a deliverable and compelling point of differentiation.

Like Southwest did in its early years, many companies fast-track this process and intuit much of the proposition themselves, at least as a starting point. Certainly, history suggests that success, and indeed failure, can result from a range of methodologies. However, that has as much to do with the fact that success is dependent upon actual execution of the brand strategy as it does with defining it. Your "big idea" can be the most compelling and interesting concept imaginable, but if you fail to inculcate it across all the various customer touch points, it will not resonate with customers.

Relating your brand values to the five classic dimensions of customer service

Once your brand values have been defined, you can run them through the ServQual filter. In this way, your branded customer service will be built on a foundation of excellent generic service, which is service quality that meets the five classic dimensions of customer service. As introduced earlier, the five components of the ServQual measurement were delineated from extensive group and survey research to let businesspeople know what customers consider good service over a range of industries—in other words, generic service.[2] Staff will then know how to deliver unique brand values on service dimensions that are fundamentally important to consumers.

1. *Reliability.* Service is carried out dependably and accurately. Emotional benefit: Customers feel they can rely on the service provider.

2. *Assuredness.* Service staff demonstrate trust and confidence. Emotional response: Customers trust the work being done and statements that are made.

3. *Tangibility.* Service staff and premises are clean and look good. Emotional judgment: Customers sense the organization takes pride in itself.

4. *Empathy.* Service staff are caring and provide individualized attention. Emotional reaction: Customers feel recognized as individuals.

5. *Responsiveness.* Service staff are willing to rapidly help customers. Emotional experience: Customers feel they are important to the organization.

ServQual applied

Let's walk through a ServQual process with a fictional service business, a real estate agency called Dream Homes. First we need to define the agency's brand vision, mission, promise, and values. Then we can relate the five ServQual components while linking them to Dream Homes' total brand space.

We'll start Dream Homes as a small operation (one broker and five agents) in a relatively large metropolis that is experiencing a real estate boom. Dream Homes' vision is to become the number one real estate brand in its city. This is not a small vision because of the stiff competition from the big national realty brands, but Dream Homes' founder is a charismatic person and sees an opportunity in a marketplace where Realtors frequently mistreat home buyers and sellers because there are so many of them. The reason Dream Homes exists—its mission—is to provide complete real estate services to help people find their dream homes, whatever their dream. The brand promise, expressed in its tagline, is "If you can dream it, we can find it." After careful study of the local marketplace, Dream Homes has chosen the following values: compatibility, honesty, attentiveness, fun, and thoroughness, which Dream Homes' founder believes most of the competitors are lacking.

The staff of Dream Homes have gone through a process of stating precisely what each of these values means in relationship to the five ServQual components of good generic service. Their (fictional) work is summarized in table 2.

Once your customer service brand space can be readily and easily described, you then need to permeate your culture with these ideas. In

Table 2. Relating brand values and ServQual

OUR BRAND VALUES	HOW WE DELIVER SERVQUAL COMPONENTS
Compatibility *We make sure that we are the right Realtors for you. We do not work with everyone. If we do not believe that our services will serve you well, we will tell you. Because we believe that buying a home is one of the most important things you will ever do, we want to make sure that when we say "we care," we mean it. We want to get to know as much about you as possible so you can find your dream home. We begin with a consulting hour so we can know you and you can know us.*	**Reliability** *Every document in our office is checked by at least one other person. We have employees who know our business and who work with us part-time. In this way, when we get backed up, we can take care of your needs instead of offering the excuse "Well, we're real busy here." We double-check our appointments so no one's time is wasted.*
Honesty *We promise to give you complete information about any property you are interested in. We will never make side deals. If your purchase or sale is quick, we will return a portion of our commission to you.*	**Assuredness** *We commit to honesty, even if it means we lose a sale. We would rather have you in the home that is best for you. We'll detail all the downsides of any property you consider, and we'll also let you know if your dream extends beyond your pocketbook. Once we commit to working for you, we'll stay with you until you find your dream home.*
Attentiveness *We promise to return all your calls within 24 hours. Period. We will always have someone in the office to talk with you 7 days a week.*	**Tangibility** *We all take responsibility for ensuring that our offices and vehicles are clean and in good working order. We have invested in good-looking office facilities. We have invested in the latest technological tools, so someone is reachable at all hours.*
Fun *Purchasing a home is a big deal. We promise to make this as much fun as possible. We want to enjoy our own work, so we pay attention to the business of creating dreams!*	**Empathy** *We take the time to get to know you. We conduct a full hour consultation before any business occurs. We want to make sure that you enjoy working with us. We are a fun-loving group of Realtors. If there is any tension in our personal relationships with clients, we can shift a client to one of our other Realtors.*
Thoroughness *Real estate is the business of details. We promise to consider any and all opportunities for you. You won't have to tell us what you want more than once. We are technological wizards and keep complete records. You'll be driven around to shop the neighborhood in clean vehicles, represented by friendly Realtors. You'll have the opportunity to visit our gorgeous offices and share English high tea service every afternoon at 4 P.M.*	**Responsiveness** *We absolutely commit to rapid responses to you. Because we are a small office, we brief each other on our individual clients so we can all pitch in and help each other when one Realtor is busy in the field.*

this way, you create brand operating rules, much like birds create flocking patterns utilizing the principles of self-organizing systems. A brand model, Inside-Out Branding, can help you visualize what steps you need to take.

Inside-out branding

TMI is the company with which we are affiliated, Janelle with TMI US and Paul with TMI New Zealand. The heart and soul of the TMI brand always has been to inspire profound behavior change so that our clients (individuals, teams, and organizations) can better meet their objectives. In order to do this, TMI as a company has paid serious attention to its own internal behaviors.

Many of TMI's consultants joined the company because of the profound impact a TMI program had on them while they were participants. They liked the experience so much that they were drawn to teach TMI's branded products. TMI has successfully pulled and pushed its consultants and staff to live the behaviors that are taught in TMI programs.

TMI: an internal analysis

One of TMI's programs, Time Manager, places an emphasis on quality that has been carefully thought through. For example, our program directors will spend hours setting up a seminar room. When they're finished, all the participant materials have been placed on tables within a defined, measurable range. The brand impact on the participants when they first walk into a room with this type of setup is persuasive that TMI is an organized company. If you visit an international TMI meeting, you will see approximately 150 people using the Time Manager planning tool, or working the same principles on Microsoft Outlook or their PDAs.

TMI also offers a program called A Complaint Is a Gift. People inside the organization really do say thank you when they hear complaints—most of the time.

Humor is highly prized as a cultural value in TMI. A lot of time is spent entertaining each other at international meetings, sometimes to the point where we fall out of our chairs with laughter. As a result, many people have been with the company for decades. TMI, while not perfect, is pretty consistently branded from the inside out.

From Time Manager workshops to culture change consulting

By the early 1980s, TMI had already achieved a remarkable brand status in Europe with the Time Manager product. So, it was not too surprising that Scandinavian Airlines (SAS) came to TMI for help with branding and changing its culture to be an on-time, business airline. This work with SAS was later recognized by the American Management Association (AMA) on the occasion of its seventy-fifth anniversary. To note the event, AMA compiled a list of the seventy-five most significant decisions its members believed helped define the very nature of management. Number one was the decision by Moses to bring the Ten Commandments down from Mount Sinai. Another of those seventy-five decisions was that made by CEO Jan Carlzon to implement TMI's company-wide service brand initiative at SAS. Every single SAS employee went through a two-day culture change program that set the stage for how the airline was to deliver the SAS brand, targeted to business travelers.

One aspect of this process that so impressed AMA was that the same message was delivered in cross-functional groups. For the very first time, a mechanic could be found sitting next to a pilot. A vice president could easily be surrounded by ticket agents and janitors. This intervention was, as far as is known, the first time (1981) that the same program messages were offered to everyone in a large, major corporation.

Part of the notoriety of this process resulted when, the following year, SAS was named the world's number one airline. What really caught everyone's attention, however, was that SAS went from a major financial loss to a huge financial profit in one year's time. The two-day TMI brand experience program focusing on individual behavior that pulled the best from people was not the only step that SAS took to change and refocus its brand. Managers led and completed 120 internally generated projects that ensured SAS delivered what it was advertising, the on-time business airline.

Approximately a year later, TMI landed the contract to educate 38,500 British Airways (BA) employees in a program called Putting People First. That phrase became government-owned BA's mantra. Prime Minister Margaret Thatcher wanted to privatize the airline and sought the highest possible stock price. A year following TMI's intervention, British Airways was named the number one airline in the world, and shortly thereafter the airline was successfully privatized. Some twenty years later, old British Airways hands still talk about the strength of the uniquely BA service culture that was created. Here's how Sir Colin Marshall, CEO during that period, described the strategy behind his decision:

> I guess the importance of brand management came home to me during my Norton Simon days, when I was responsible for Hunt-Wesson. That experience . . . helped me realize that instilling a brand culture is very important in a service business because a service business is all about serving people who have values, ideals, and feelings. It helped me realize that we needed to see the product not simply as a seat but more comprehensively as an experience being orchestrated across the airline. That orchestration was the brand.[3]

Inside-out brand model

While conducting this work with SAS and BA, TMI began laying the groundwork for a model that today we call Inside-Out Branding. It is a model that spells out the requirements of successful culture change projects and also helps explain why so many customer service interventions and branding projects fail.

Quadrants 1 and 2 in figure 4 represent organizations whose business models require limited customer-staff interaction, such as Coca-Cola and Morton Salt, both dominated by manufacturing, distribution, and brand development. Most consumers of Coca-Cola, which because of its brand differentiation belongs in quadrant 2, never interact with representatives from the Coca-Cola Company. To begin with, Coke rarely tastes different, bottle to bottle or can to can. About the only time consumers have problems with Coca-Cola is when they get a flat one dispensed through a tap. Coca-Cola and Morton Salt have effectively used traditional brand marketing communication (marcom) strategies to differentiate their brands to the general public. This has saved them from performing like a nondifferentiated quadrant 1 commodity.

Figure 4. Inside-out brand model

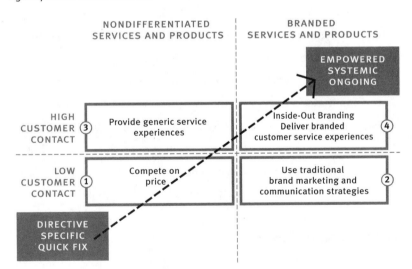

Marcom typically emphasizes product promises, or pull marketing. Quality is implied if not explicitly stated. Customers are told what to expect from a product. If done well, marcom "delivers" customers to try products and services. Manufacturers of products such as Coca-Cola pay greater attention (and advertising dollars) to the messages that entice customers to decide to make a first-time purchase than they do to creating an experience where on-brand service delivery helps cement repeat sales. Once the product is in hand, continued advertising entices the customer to make repeat purchases.

The return on investment (ROI) statistics that advertising agencies cite regarding successful marcom interventions are almost exclusively about quadrant 2 products. Quadrant 2 is where most of the world's successful brands can be categorized. Of the top 100 brands, only 25 are service brands. Yet the service economy accounts for over two-thirds of the developed world's gross domestic product.[4] We predict this 25-to-75 ratio will change in the next decade as more and more service companies become adept at branding their service and thereby build brand equity.

Three defining market challenges

Today's quadrant 2 marketing world is affected by three defining market challenges prevalent since the early 1990s.

1. *The standout challenge.* It is increasingly difficult and expensive to make a brand stand out from the crowd today solely using advertisements. So many products are essentially the same that the consumer has come to the conclusion if one brand is not available, then another will do just fine. To be noticed, some ads are so clever it is impossible not to watch them on television. Their cleverness, however, sometimes makes the messages so obscure that the viewer has no idea what product or promise is being advertised. Inundation

marketing as practiced in the past has less impact today than it did in the past.

2. *The proliferation challenge.* The sites where advertising can be placed have exploded in number. Consumers see and hear ads everywhere—on television, on radio, in magazines, in newspapers, on moving vehicles, all over the Internet, flashing on elevator video displays, embedded in movies, on flyers, on billboards, on products, and even cut into hairstyles. The once-dominant major television channels are being challenged by strong cable stations, and most homes receive hundreds of channels. When promotion includes hiring young people to stand at a stop light and loudly discuss a certain product so passersby can overhear the conversation, then *proliferation* is probably too mild of a word to describe what has happened to marketing.

3. *The consumer cynicism challenge.* Many consumers are cynical about the sheer volume of advertising messages luring them in a certain direction. The public has become much more educated about its consumer rights, and it expects advertising promises to be delivered.[5]

Quadrants 3 and 4 describe organizations whose products and services have highly concentrated personal customer contact, including retail stores, the hospitality industry, technology companies with a great deal of customer technical support, professional services, health care, education, banking and finance, government, insurance, and entertainment. These types of industries have little chance at success if they do not pay attention to how their brand is delivered by staff.

Because of the higher margins possible with differentiated offerings, most companies would obviously prefer to occupy either quadrant 2 or quadrant 4. The alternative is to compete primarily on price. Businesses that sell their products with limited personal customer contact can use direct and specific quick marketing fixes to gain market share and build brand equity. Businesses that want to create a branded service experience, however, have a much harder row to plow. Efforts must be ongoing. They must be systemic, impacting every aspect of the organization. And they depend upon delivery by empowered staff. In short, to succeed in quadrant 4, businesses need to brand their service experiences in very clever ways. They must also generate a service culture with committed staff and effective service delivery processes.

Classic marketing mistakes when defining brand space

Many marketing professionals believe that branding is predominantly, or even exclusively, a marketing function. Furthermore, they see branding residing exclusively in the marketing department. We recall talking with a group of executives whose senior vice president of marketing was not on board with the service branding effort the company was instituting, especially as it was being encroached on by operational staff. At one point in an animated discussion about brand space, he asserted, "What are you talking about? Our *brand* is our logo." His comments were met with gasps and then stunned silence from his colleagues around the company.

They were light-years ahead of him. He had clearly missed the point of what this nonmarketing, branding team was attempting to do. The team would have better agreed with UK Renault Brand Manager Marx Waller, who put it this way: "Brand management is essentially about culture change."[6] Unfortunately for the vice president of marketing, the CEO of the company heard about his remarks, and he is no longer with that company.

Let us review how we have described a brand: an identity and reputation shaped by the beliefs that consumers have about products, services, or organizations. Such beliefs are formed as a result of all the interactions that the public has with the product, staff, and organization. This imperative must be a critical consideration for marketing specialists within service organizations with a high level of customer interaction.

Indeed, we believe that the influence that each and every staff member can have in shaping the perceptions about a brand is becoming progressively more important. Today's customers are able to interact directly with a much wider range of employees within organizations. One telling example of this expanded communication is e-mail, a massive means of communication that is often informal and colloquial. Every one of these interactions can have an impact on shaping perceptions about a brand.

While branding as a concept is peeking its head out of marketing departments, in order to be fully communicated, branding must reside "everywhere" in organizations. Fiscally responsible organizations must use the power of brand to differentiate their products and service offerings from competitors'.[7] This requires, at a minimum, intense communication and cooperation between marketing (to lead the branding effort externally) and other departments (to lead the branding effort internally).[8]

Stretch: finding your space between brand push and pull

Because employees spend enormous amounts of time at work, they potentially have a highly involved relationship with their brand employer. By using the complementary dimensions of *push* and *pull* (brand stretch) and simultaneously paying attention to the brand power tools of likability, reinforcement, and consistency (see chapter 5), brand promises and values can motivate staff and create brand service momentum.

- *Push.* When brand values have been carefully developed and linked to business strategy, they support and add credibility to the brand.

They explain how and why the organization can lay claim to its brand promises. Pusher (as he prefers to be called) Mark Di Somma suggests that brand values "act as a personality litmus, ensuring the company remains focused on what's important."[9] When staff live and work by these reinforced values, delivery of brand promises becomes possible.

Brand values provide a framework for designing and implementing integrated systems, processes, measurements, and rewards that will align employee behaviors to the service culture that underpins the brand. This *pushes* staff from the inside to adopt the skills, attitudes, and standards necessary to meet customers' needs within a consistent delivery space, as in, for example, "guaranteed overnight delivery."

- *Pull.* The brand promise—who we are and what we stand for—is an expression of a company's vision in its simplest form. It acts as a unifying force across all parts of the organization. As employees become emotionally engaged with the brand they represent, they become *pulled* toward it. If the brand has strength and excitement, it gives staff a sense of identity, a feeling of belonging, and makes them feel positive about going to work. It also provides a clear sense of common purpose, a strong customer focus, and an orientation toward the future. This becomes the impetus to pull on-brand behavior so staff want to be the very best they can for their customers.

People who work in strongly branded companies understand what the company is promising, because the promise is actively promoted internally. Then, every time service representatives see their brand presented in advertisements, marketing literature, or billboards, it builds their self-esteem and reminds them of the promises being made to customers so they are *pulled* to deliver it. It helps build commitment.

This influence is not to be underestimated. When Paul worked with a New Zealand company called Baycorp, it faced a major challenge in shifting perceptions about the brand. The public primarily knew Baycorp for the debt collection and credit referencing services it had provided for twenty-five years. This perception was out of touch with the reality of the technology- and data-based business solutions company Baycorp had become. Yet the lingering and disparaging reputation as a debt collector dramatically impacted staff. The brand had never been actively managed. As a result, staff beliefs were primarily shaped by what outsiders thought about them. If you tell employees often enough that they are a sore or parasite on society, it is not long before the service culture starts to reflect that.

Simply pushing from the inside to change these destructive behaviors could achieve only so much. However, when Baycorp combined a powerful brand marketing strategy—deployed externally and internally—that reflected the current reality of what the company offered, the self-esteem of staff and the behaviors that they deemed to be on-brand improved rapidly and significantly.

Ideally, if brands are to provide such an impetus to shift employee behavior, they need an element of stretch. Even though the goal is to align service delivery with the brand promise, an organization's brand promise does not have to be exactly reflected in employee behavior. The *pull* or aspiration can hint at something better than today's reality, but not to an extreme. After all, we know that when we buy a new car, young shapely women dressed in bikinis do not normally drape themselves over our shiny automobile, as they frequently do in ads. Likewise, the *push* or standards can be challenging to deliver all the time, but again, not to an extreme.

Rather than talk about the disparity that often exists between brand values and branded service delivery, we can more appropriately talk about tension or *stretch* between the best way we can represent our brand (pull) and our minimum standards of brand delivery (push). Brand stretch, when carefully deployed, has the inherent capacity to simultaneously push and pull employees to show them what to do and how to do it. The right degree of stretch keeps staff on their toes to meet the challenge of delivering the brand promise.

Too much pull and employees give up and become cynical. "Sure, this is what our advertising says, but actually we are nothing like that." From a customer service perspective, "continuous delight" and "constantly exceeding expectations" are examples of pull aspirations that are simply too high. Too much push and employees also give up and become cynical. "There's no way we can do that all the time." For example, 100 percent satisfaction guaranteed is too high a push target.

What is the right amount of stretch? It varies from situation to situation depending upon the type of culture, momentum already created, and how committed management is to supporting the change required. However, as a rule of thumb, if the feeling of most staff is "Yes, when we are near our best, that's us," then you are probably in the ballpark.

One of the best examples of push and pull we have seen is that of the World Bank. Its mission is to end world poverty. There is a lot of pull in that mission, and absolute fulfillment would seem unachievable. Yet few of us would disagree that any significant progress toward it is a worthwhile achievement, which is why World Bank staff are remarkably in touch with that aspiration on a day-to-day basis. On the push side, the World Bank has established high quality standards that encourage its delivery of services to the local agencies it serves.

In so many organizations, however, we have seen millions of dollars invested in the right marketing literature. We have also seen not a penny spent on engaging staff so they really understand and begin to live the brand and values. In these vacuum circumstances, staff, just like customers, develop their own beliefs about the brand (we're untrustworthy, we do not deliver, we frequently disappoint, we lack integrity) and what is required of them.

off-brand

Some time ago, one of New Zealand's leading banks ran a major television advertising campaign with the tagline "Knowledge Makes the Difference." The bank was implicitly saying it had more information, ideas, and expertise that allowed it to better meet the specific needs of individual customers than its competitors.

One of our colleagues heard the bank's radio ad, which announced a free "Hot Tips" brochure for rental property investors was available to anybody who dropped by a branch. Although he was not a customer of the bank, our friend was hooked by the offer. He stopped by to pick up both bank literature and the brochure. To his dismay, not only was the brochure not available, but a very pleasant customer service representative did not "have any knowledge" about it. "They never tell us about these things," she said apologetically. Needless to say, this prospective customer was not swayed to set up an account with the "knowledge makes the difference" bank.

Could good generic customer service have taken care of our colleague's experience with this bank? The bank clerk, after all, was not rude. She was not particularly slow. She was not incompetent. She simply had no knowledge about the free brochure—knowledge that linked to the bank's brand tagline and advertised messages. Through no fault of her own she delivered off-brand service. Based on her comment, this type of situation had apparently happened to her before, and she was no longer pulled or motivated to go out of her way to find the requested information.

American Express is remarkably good at defining its brand attributes. One aspect of a recent brand message is "Do More." However, it's clear the message hasn't been integrated at a customer service delivery level. A recent telephone call we made to handle a billing issue concluded with a barrage of obviously scripted sales statements for other services that were read so fast they were barely intelligible. The feeling we were left with was not "do more," as American Express wants to help its customers achieve, but rather one of imposition. No doubt, this effort was driven by the marketing department with little regard to how the messages would be delivered and how the customer would hear this barrage. Was it bad service? Not necessarily. Was it off-brand? No doubt. Listening to at least three minutes of sales messages, which were repeated twice, helps few people "do more." The time has come for marketing departments to stop delegating sales tasks to other departments without regard to impact on delivery. Staff will comply; they will plow through such messages but with little regard as to how they are received by consumers.

Signals of an on-brand culture

How can you tell if your organizational culture is delivering its brand DNA? Some signals are industry dependent, but the general signals listed in table 3 can help highlight areas that require attention.

What does your organization's culture mean to people who come to your establishment—whatever that purpose may be? Does it symbolize anything different from a competitor down the road? Perhaps even more important, what does your organization mean to the people who work there? Is your brand DNA being lived and expressed? Inside-Out Branding not only encompasses the customers' interactions with staff, it also includes every internal and external process that shapes how any person, staff, or supplier interacts with your organization. In his book, *Corporate Religion,* Jesper Kunde pinpoints the role of corporate cultures in strong brands: "In the future, building strong market positions will be about building companies with a strong personality and corporate soul."[10]

TMI worked with the Hong Kong offices of two major U.S. multinational corporations that both blatantly violated copyright laws by duplicating our materials without our permission. When they would not stop, we ultimately threatened that we would report this violation to their U.S. corporate offices. That got their attention and their cooperation, because in both cases violating copyright laws is in direct conflict with their explicitly stated global corporate values. Every time we do business with these companies, we remember how their employees tried to cheat us in such a heavy-handed manner and violated copyright laws with impunity. Even though this happened while TMI was a supplier to them, it is part of our total brand experience, and it affects our evaluation when we are their customer.

One of the leading providers of credit references and debt recovery services in Australia and Asia contacted thousands of consumers and other businesses every day to remind them of both their legal and moral obligations to meet financial commitments. Yet this company had a reputation among its suppliers for slow payment. Regardless of whether this was the practice because of employee behavior, poor processes, or a strategic decision to delay payment, the fact remains that it undermined the integrity of the company's brand. Word spreads.

Human resources as a strategic brand partner

It is possible to make the argument that branding actually lives more in the human resources department than it does in the marketing

Table 3. Signals of on- and off-brand cultures

OFF-BRAND CULTURE	ON-BRAND CULTURE
Indicators that the brand DNA has not penetrated the organizational culture	*Signals that the brand DNA has penetrated the organizational culture*
The brand is considered to be in the domain of marketers.	*The brand is understood and valued and provides meaning to everyone.*
The brand is developed in isolation from the service culture.	*The organization's brand has been deliberately created as it relates to service delivery.*
Senior management pays little attention to the strategic and operational impact of the brand.	*The brand provides guidelines and context for all service experience touch points.*
The brand is largely seen as irrelevant to daily business functions.	*All parts of the organization understand the unique proposition of the brand and their role in delivering it.*
Performance measures do not incorporate delivery of brand-aligned behaviors.	*Performance assessment explicitly measures congruence of service delivery and the brand.*
Brand decisions are made across the organization based upon personal preference or short-term considerations.	*Brand decisions are strategically integrated into all parts of the organization and reflect long-term plans.*
Leadership behavior contradicts the brand.	*Senior managers understand the brand and reflect it in their own behavior.*
Recruitment is driven primarily by intelligence, skills, and experience without regard to the brand.	*People are recruited for their capacity to deliver experiences in line with the brand.*

department. A corollary to this statement is that the key audience for the marketing department is employees, who are at least as important as paying customers.

Bill Oden, one of TMI's consultants, is prone to say that "Service branding in organizations is not about a way of doing certain things. Customer service branding is about a certain way of doing everything by everyone." And who better than both marketing and human resource departments (and training departments if they are housed separately from HR) to shape and communicate this "certain way"? If this is to be done, marketing professionals need to act more as integrators of the brand for the entire organization. And HR professionals need to act more as strategic business partners instead of personnel administrators.

An HR department can take many steps to redesign itself to match the organizational brand. From employment charts and policies and procedures to training programs, companies intentionally or unintentionally need to work at making their staff act, look, sound, and even feel that "certain way." Unfortunately, if not carefully and constantly assessed and nurtured, these efforts can wind up as veneers with no lasting impact on customer interactions.

An organization that designs its customer service to align with its brand must start from the premise that the brand will be displayed and delivered by staff who are influenced and inspired by their managers and supervisors. Employees not only must feel pride in the quality of their products, but they must also work within and feel engaged by the system that helps them deliver branded service experiences.

When an organization is branded from the inside out, managers will have a context by which to filter their supervisory behaviors toward their staff. Staff will also then be more likely to understand when service delivery does not match the brand position. When this happens, based on a solid description of brand DNA, all will know on a daily basis when they are off-brand, and they will know what they need to do to get on-brand.

5

Brand Power Tools: Likability, Reinforcement, and Consistency

The most powerful brands are robust and multifaceted, while at the same time they are precisely defined. Likability, reinforcement, and consistency are three key power tools that marketers use to achieve brand dominance. These power tools possess equal power for service managers when they are applied to service experiences. *Through consistent reinforcement* of an offering that is both *liked* and *appreciated,* a brand will engage consumers.

Power tool 1: likability

Most of the research conducted about likability deals with what is required to get customers to purchase. Marketing experts have long known that if customers like your advertisements, they will more likely remember you and feel better about your products and services. Likability is inextricably involved in how people respond to each other, to ideas, and to brands.

On the surface, likability seems simple enough: humor and warm feelings.[1] But likability is also influenced by variables such as the context and medium in which ads are shown and whether the person watching is a "high involvement" person or "low involvement" person.[2]

Since people seem to like things depending on who they are and when and where they see things, ads need to be checked for likability in relationship to when and where they will be seen before a huge amount of money is spent to display them.

Likability within customer service also needs to be measured on a regular basis. As we seem to have trained consumers to say they are satisfied whether they are or not, perhaps we would gain better customer feedback if we simply asked them if they like the way they were treated. Satisfaction and likability are two extremely different indicators. In fact, many companies have confused customer inertia with satisfaction, thinking "If our customers aren't leaving us, then they must be satisfied." When customers don't relish their experiences with a brand, they will not be as involved. Even if they aren't leaving at the moment, they are primed to be snatched by a competitor.

Because likability has not yet been researched as a branded customer service deliverable, we can only extrapolate from the research that has been conducted on advertising. Christine Freuchte, CME Kid-Com general manager, points out that marketers know likability of ads strictly by itself does not generate desire.[3] Likability sparks interest. Interest must then be linked to preferences, needs, or concerns to inspire desire. Customer service can be an ideal medium in which to inspire desire.

What does likability mean in customer service delivery? Obviously, every brand will have a different behavioral answer to this question. With generic service, likability might mean remembering names; with branded customer service, it could mean using titles or formal names to reinforce your sense of exclusiveness. With generic service, likability generally means thanking your customers; with branded service, it could mean sending a personalized thank-you note or gift that reflects your brand—such as a donation to a charity with which your brand is affiliated. With generic service, likability might mean paying attention;

with branded customer service, it could mean paying attention in ways that relate to your brand promise, such as repeating information in a set way (such as Starbucks does) so you make sure you get everything correct the first time. When customers like what happened in service delivery, an even stronger desire for the brand occurs if that service experience reinforces the brand's identity.[4]

Power tool 2: reinforcement

The second brand power tool, reinforcement, is a process of strengthening consumer perceptions. Without reinforcement, a brand image is easily diluted and is also jarring to the customer.

---

off-brand

Blockbuster Video's mission is "To help people transform ordinary nights into Blockbuster nights by being their complete source for movies and games."

With a mission statement like this, empowerment plays a big part in accomplishing it. At many Blockbuster checkout counters you will even see a card informing customers that every Blockbuster employee is empowered to do what is necessary to ensure your happiness. It's a selling point, part of Blockbuster's value proposition.

Author Shel Horowitz was so excited about Blockbuster's position on empowerment that he wanted to include it as a positive example in his new book, Principled Profit. *However, when—in order to save herself eight extra miles of driving—Shel's wife called their local Blockbuster store and asked if she could return a video two hours late at no extra charge, the person in charge told her he had no authority to do that.*

Most of us would derisively say, "It figures. They say one thing and do another. Their signs are just so many words." In this case, reinforcement of the brand was dashed to the extent that Shel's entire perception of Blockbuster has changed.

Having a practice that does not allow every employee to make an exception to policies could be a good, reasonable service policy. But if being able to make immediate decisions is part of "transform(ing) ordinary nights into Blockbuster nights," then empowerment is essential. In this case, telling the customer no would be better than saying "I have no authority to do that." No may not be the answer the customer wants, but at least it doesn't fly in the face of the brand promise. Any question regarding tonight's video entertainment has to be settled immediately to reinforce the brand promise of Blockbuster happiness. In this case, if a form has to be filled out or a higher-level manager contacted to make an exception to policy, off-brand service has been delivered and the brand is compromised.

Power tool 3: consistency

The third brand power tool is consistency and is the major challenge for customer service. If customers are to return to places of business they like, they need to feel as if they are returning to a familiar place. The brand needs to have a repeated feeling of familiarity about it. As Tim Ambler, with the London Business School says, "Brands earn their reputation for reliability, not from a rapid investment in communications, but from providing consistent satisfaction over many years."[5]

Because customer service involves human exchange, people who deliver customer service will always struggle with consistency. If too consistent, customer service loses its ability to make an impact on us.

If every waiter says, "Enjoy," before we begin to eat our meal, this attempt at friendliness can become extremely unlikable. Yet some restaurants actually script their staff to say precisely that.

In order to believe that the other person is authentic, most people expect some variety in their human interactions. As University of Chicago physics professor John Rader Platt says, "The needs of man, if life is to survive, are usually said to be four—air, water, food, and in the severe climates, protection. But it is becoming clear today that [there is a fifth need] the need for novelty—the need, throughout our waking life, for continuous variety in the external stimulation of our eyes, ears, sense organs, and all our nervous network."[6]

Fortunately, if we let service representatives be themselves, they will not repeat themselves over and over again. They get tired of spouting mindless repetition as much as customers do listening to it. And they don't want to sound like mere mimics of their colleagues unless it's part of a ritual. If given a sense of a brand's personality or tone of voice, people will find creative ways to individually express themselves within the brand's personality and still create the novelty and authenticity that we expect in human interactions. Remember, for branded service to be consistent, it does not have to be identical. It merely has to be recognizable.[7] This is particularly challenging for organizations that have merged service offerings to their customers, as in the case of the off-brand service below.

---

off-brand (AND HORRIBLE GENERIC SERVICE)

Janelle purchased an around-the-world ticket on United Airlines in business class, spending the extra money because she wanted protection for what would be inevitable changes to her itinerary written with the multiple airlines of United's Star Alliance. The brand promise of the Star Alliance is that if one airline doesn't have a desk in a particular city, passengers can go to any of the Star Alliance partners and be helped. The alliance is a great idea and adds a lot of extra value to customers, but the promise has to be delivered to work.

Sure enough, one ticket change in the middle of Janelle's trip necessitated rewriting her entire ticket. On an around-the-world fare, this involved recalculating distances, taxes, and so on. The adventure started in Zagreb, Croatia, where the Lufthansa ticket agent, while personable, didn't have enough time before Janelle's flight left for Warsaw to reissue the ticket. The ticket agent, however, said she would send a special note to the Lufthansa Warsaw airport desk with all the change details programmed into the computer for easy pickup. Janelle left for Warsaw with a happy heart, confident that the Star Alliance brand concept worked!

Late on a Friday afternoon, however, the two Lufthansa agents at the Warsaw airport refused to help! They told Janelle that the UAL (Lufthansa's partner) locator codes and ticket calculation price changes were "worthless," even though the changes had been entered by Lufthansa in Croatia.

Janelle asked about the promised note from the helpful lady in Zagreb. They said it wasn't there and that a note wouldn't have been enough in any case; the woman from Zagreb should have called them to see that this was okay with them! When Janelle asked how she could possibly be expected to know this, they shrugged their shoulders. They told Janelle she would have to go to Austrian Airlines, her next carrier, even though all the airlines on her itinerary are partners in the Star Alliance program.

Austrian Airlines service staff couldn't have been more helpful. They did everything and did it fast. They also indicated that the

Zagreb note was in the file and apologized for their partner. New ticket in hand, Janelle marched back to the Lufthansa desk to tell them what she had learned. The woman acknowledged that she had lied. She said she just didn' t feel like reissuing the ticket! It was too much work in her estimation and of no benefit to Lufthansa.

All it took was two women with off-brand behavior, and the Star Alliance brand—several airlines to help you while you fly just one—was dashed.

Clearly, this service was appalling as well as off-brand, a lethal combination for brand building. Janelle will tell you that the bad service, which she actually found so horrible as to be entertaining, stung less than the damage done to her brand concept of Star Alliance. On her next flight to Europe, Janelle booked herself on United to London. She then switched out of the Star Alliance system to her next destination rather than give her business to Lufthansa.

Richard Branson, founder and CEO of Virgin (the huge British brand ranging from Virgin Airways to Virgin Records and dozens of companies in between) writes passionately about branding as individual human behavior:[8]

> The idea that business is strictly a numbers affair has always struck me as preposterous. It is my conviction that what we call "shareholder value" is best defined by how strongly employees and customers feel about your brand. Nothing seems more obvious to me that a product or service only becomes a brand when it is imbued with profound values that translate into fact and feeling that employees can project and customers can embrace.[9]

Branson's words are an ultimatum to both brand and customer service experts. He advocates that "profound values" must be defined in advance, strategically linked to brand positions, and promoted to staff. Then comes Branson's challenge: "translate into feelings that employees project and customers embrace." We believe this challenge can be met.

6

Culture Change:
The Bedrock of
Brand Development

In the business best seller *Good to Great,* Jim Collins identifies three interrelated attributes common to companies that have been able to make sustainable leaps in performance. They include identifying

- what the company can be best at in the world
- what best ignites the passion of its people
- how its economics work best[1]

The first and second of these "bests" are directly connected to brand and organizational culture. Sustained performance excellence happens when brands are connected to what staff do best. Branding can also spark passion by channeling ambition, creating a clear vision, and building a sense of identity and purpose for everyone who is a part of it. Economic strategy—Collins's third interrelated attribute—creates the financial context in which branding occurs. All three attributes are aspects of organizational culture.

The power of corporate culture and brands

For many years, astute managers have recognized that they must actively manage and foster their organizational cultures. When *Fortune* magazine released the results of its 1995 Corporate Reputations Survey, it underscored the point: "There is a growing realization that companies cannot live by numbers alone . . . the one thing that set the top ranking companies in the survey apart is their robust cultures."[2]

Culture as a concept has been applied to organizations for decades. Intense public consideration began in 1982, when Tom Peters and Robert Waterman wrote *In Search of Excellence.* They argued that culture, consisting of behaviors and beliefs, is the glue that holds organizations together.[3] When a company's culture is strong, a consistent set of behaviors and values is evident across the majority of managers and employees.

With the growing list of corporate failures in the early 2000s exemplified by Worldcom, Enron, Parmalat, and HIH Insurance (Australia), this glue is coming under even greater scrutiny. Increasingly, stakeholders of all types—stockholders, suppliers, customers, and employees—question the integrity, transparency, and quality of organizations with which they deal. Can organizational self-reports be trusted? Can executives be believed when they say they will do something? Does the organization operate in a manner that is consistent with the values it espouses and the brand promises it makes?

Regulatory authorities are jumping into the act, holding managers accountable to the company values and cultures they espouse. A recent claim was brought by the New Zealand Employment Relations Authority against EDS, the giant information technology outsourcing company, for unfairly laying off staff. The authority criticized EDS for "its gross failure to honor its own values system," including "value and respect for the individual" and "keep[ing] lines of communication open."[4]

Many business leaders maintain that their most sustainable competitive advantage is corporate spirit, employee engagement, and a belief throughout the organization in what it is trying to achieve. We are living in an age when intangible values are identified as key indicators of success. It is also a period when the most productive workers tend to be those who are engaged with and connected to the soul of the organization. It is estimated that a recent and minor drop in employee engagement in Singapore, for example, costs that economy between $4.9 billion and $6.7 billion annually.[5]

Some people still hold the misplaced view that culture is simply about the soft side of a company, that culture is solely about creating a caring and nurturing environment for employees. The reality is that culture is actually about performance, an idea validated by studies that show a strong link between company culture and financial results. Lyle Spencer, researcher and emotional intelligence expert, concludes that while results vary from company to company, in general every 1 percent improvement in service climate delivers a 2 percent increase in revenue.[6]

A strong culture, by itself, is not a guarantee of economic success. In fact, it may be counterproductive under certain conditions. John Kotter and James Heskett explain that "Strategy is simply the logic for how to achieve movement in some direction. The beliefs and practices called for in a strategy may be compatible with a firm's culture, or they may not. When they are not, the company finds it difficult to implement the strategy necessary."[7]

The nature of values and behaviors that typify the culture of a company are therefore more important than its strength. A successful culture is adaptive to the environment in which it exists. If the culture values customers highly and directs change to serve their needs, then the organization will be more adaptive. This is why a brand can be a powerful conduit for culture change. A brand can be seen as an expression of the relationship between the company and its stakeholders. A brand that has been well thought through will reflect the overlap between the needs of customers, the industry in terms of product or service capabilities, and the company culture. In contrast, according to Kotter and Heskett, companies that have strong cultures but are poor performers lack this outward focus. Instead, they act more out of self-interest, are characterized by bureaucratic centralization and insularity, and are often arrogant.[8]

Changing corporate cultures

A strong culture happens when everyone in a company understands and does what it takes to deliver the productivity, relations, and quality consistent with its brand promise. Indeed, in the current age of integrated branding, organizational culture is often referred to as the internal brand. In these terms, an *internal brand* is the set of organizational values that are linked to the external brand promise, with internal processes, systems, and behaviors reflecting these values.

When the values of organizations are effectively interwoven into the sinew of organizational behavior, they can provide clearer guidance for employees on how to behave and operate than HR policy manuals can. Paul recalls a workshop where ideas about HR mandates covering work practices were being explained. During a break he overheard a conversation between employees in which one said, "Those things will never happen, it's not the way things are done around here." That particular person had been with the organization for just seven weeks, and he could already see what was real and what was wishful thinking by HR.

Regardless of what corporate executives state publicly, the beliefs and behaviors of most employees are quickly and profoundly influenced by the existing culture of a company. Sam Walton, founder of Wal-Mart, the world's biggest retailer, was known to say that it takes only a week or two before employees begin treating customers the same way as they are treated by their employer.[9]

This presents both a challenge and an opportunity. The dynamic impact of culture on brand development demonstrates the risks of a top-down approach to organizational culture change. When mandated from the top, change is often met with significant resistance. The failure to align organizational behavior with desired values often occurs because the root determinants of behavior have not been considered. Gaining commitment to values demands dealing with the deeply embedded and widely held beliefs that sit at the subconscious level of a company.

Here's a telling example. Some years ago the New Zealand Fire Service decided to shift its focus from "putting out fires" to "fire prevention." The fire service emphasized educating the public about the causes and consequences of fires. It encouraged the use of smoke detectors and sprinkler systems. To reflect the new direction and brand, this shift required redirecting resources, changing operational processes, and adjusting employment relations.

Although for most of the public this was an entirely rational shift consistent with the purpose of the fire service, it met with significant resistance from the bulk of firefighters. The new direction was inconsistent with their subconscious organizational beliefs about the fire service and their role in it. They had joined the fire service for the challenge of firefighting to save lives and property. In between emergencies, they saw their role as waiting in readiness. Years of disharmony between management and staff followed this attempted brand shift.

Such experiences teach us that leaders of organizations need to develop approaches where change is shaped through and by people, not in spite of them. Too often management forgets that shifting employees to a different path is better achieved through inclusion and inspiration, rather than insistence. Consequently, when leaders want to create genuine culture change, they need to ask three questions about the proposed solution:

- Has the defined change been coherently derived from and integrated with the company's business strategy?

- Are we using an engaging, intelligent, and inspiring approach to gain buy-in from staff and management?
- How is the culture to be maintained and supported after initial change intervention(s)?

Culture change and inside-out branding

While every company by default has a culture, the tricky part is developing one that proactively supports its brand objectives. This culture imperative goes to the heart of one of the most difficult and ongoing management challenges: How does management take developed brand strategies and effectively execute them through staff at all levels in such a way that on-brand behaviors become instinctive?

Organizational development consultants normally begin the process of culture change by defining and identifying desired behaviors. Operational processes such as performance management, remuneration and recognition, and recruitment are then aligned with these values.

Inside-Out Branding, as outlined in chapter 4, has a different starting point for expressing business strategy, the brand proposition. It defines a set of carefully chosen values that a customer must experience to conclude that the brand promise was delivered. The values can then be used to harmonize internal processes from recruitment through customer service and everything in between.

While the terminology is relatively new, culture change is also very dependent on a high level of organizational *emotional intelligence* (EI).[10] When a company is emotionally intelligent, it communicates effectively, treats people appropriately, and is able to get through rough spots without serious fallout. EI includes abilities such as self-management and self-motivation. It deals with how employees relate to each other through teamwork and interpersonal communication.

Under conditions of high emotional sensitivity, internal service improves, which, in turn, bubbles up to the surface of the company and ripples out to customers in the form of improved customer service. However, if organizational functions are changed and shaped without consideration of the profound values of the brand, by the time customer experiences are impacted by these changes, they are often generic, perhaps even off-brand and not unique compared to other companies.

Brand study: Vodafone New Zealand

In 1998, the global telecommunications corporation Vodafone established itself in the New Zealand (NZ) marketplace by acquiring the subsidiary operations of Bell South. Bell South had been fighting hard for years to establish a market presence within NZ but remained very much a secondary player to the national provider, Telecom Mobile New Zealand. When Bell South was acquired, its market share in the cellular phone market was a modest 19 percent. An internal brand consultant who worked on the Vodafone NZ project reports that at that time the prevailing viewpoint of staff could be summarized as "How can we possibly compete with Telecom Mobile NZ?"

To justify its initial investment and ongoing capital expenditure, Vodafone needed to grow. The new board and management recognized what seemed to be an insurmountable challenge: how to compete against Telecom Mobile NZ with product or technology advances. The presence of Telecom Mobile NZ was so strong, it didn't matter that Vodafone NZ had the might of a multinational corporation behind them.

Jan Mottram, with the Vodafone NZ human resources department, put it this way: "We realized that the only way to create a sustainable point of differentiation was to focus on how customers felt about our brand. That meant becoming a values-based organization."[11]

Vodafone NZ management decided to become a business of consumer experiences as much as it was a seller of cellular phone services. It recognized that there was huge potential in the rapidly emerging youth and young adult market, which needed to be approached in a specific experiential way.

Part of the process included an analysis of the market from the outside in, to get a clear understanding of what consumers within Vodafone NZ's target market wanted to feel as a result of their experiences with the brand. From there a set of inspirational values was developed: zesty, your call, simple and clever, and tribe. These defined the brand persona and overlaid another set of foundation values, including integrity, excellence, and supportive.

Based on market research, Vodafone NZ management knew that customers embraced its newly defined inspirational values, so the next step was to get staff to project them. The branding process began with Vodafone NZ leadership to ensure they were powerful brand spokespeople for the company. This meant each manager had to develop a clear understanding of the organization he or she wanted to create. The process included asking managers to align their personal values with Vodafone NZ's values. They were forcefully asked for a commitment to live and communicate Vodafone NZ's values explicitly in all their actions and activities.

Vodafone NZ then worked to integrate these values into all elements of the business. Strategies and initiatives included the following:

- *A heavy emphasis on engagement with staff.* A specifically designed brand induction program was run entirely by Vodafone NZ's executive team. The program focused on how each part of the business fit with the culture and the brand.

- *A comprehensive internal communications program to keep the company's messages alive.* Every message was infused with the brand and values, including briefings to staff on strategy and communication of company results that were themed, inspirational events.

- *Changes in the physical work environment to reflect the brand and culture.* Every space was looked at, including office areas, call centers, and special rooms where staff relax (the Chill Room) or have fun (the Thrill Room). Even the most senior executives began to work in an open plan environment with their staff.

• *Modifications in strategies, policies, and processes.* These progressive changes supported and reinforced the unique brand and culture to which Vodafone NZ aspired. HR focused on three key brand-related elements: business needs assessment, employee-company alignment, and creation of passion so that people want to contribute.

Vodafone NZ managers now fundamentally believe that if the company is not living the brand, it is losing customers. When employees make decisions, interact with each other, and deal with customers, the company wants staff to give their values priority. Vodafone is clear in wanting everyone to be on-brand at all times; it has become intolerant of behavior that is out of sync with its values.

While the company sees this as an ongoing journey, it has already achieved much. Vodafone NZ is one of the strongest employment brands in New Zealand today, with employee turnover having fallen by a third. A recent staff survey demonstrated the high degree of engagement staff feel about working for Vodafone NZ.[12]

• Overall satisfaction and engagement (84 percent)
• Importance of passion for customers (97 percent)
• Importance of passion for results (97 percent)
• Pride in Vodafone NZ (96 percent)
• Role in supporting company strategy (88 percent)

Jan Mottram points to the reactions of employees when they join the company as a powerful anecdotal indicator of their success. Typically, new employees say that working at Vodafone NZ is exactly how they perceived it to be before they joined the company.

Has it delivered value? The results speak for themselves. Vodafone NZ has increased its market share from 19 to 53 percent, and brand recognition has increased from 3 to 99 percent. Vodafone NZ ascribes much of this success to its values-based organization and brand strategy. Now, Telecom Mobile NZ finds itself wondering how it can possibly compete with Vodafone NZ.

7

Communicating to Ensure Brand Resonance

How management communicates to employees really does matter. It is a critical key to any organizational culture and provides the foundation for the understanding and feeling that employees hold toward their brand. Brand-integrated employee communications programs not only keep the key brand messages alive internally through repetition but—when done well—also shape the language of the branded service culture. To accomplish this, internal communication about the brand needs to be both strategic and creative in the way it is developed and implemented.

Recognition of the key role that employee communication plays as a strategic management tool can be traced back at least twenty-five years, when Thomas F. Gilbert wrote his classic book on managing and motivating people, *Human Competence.* Gilbert did not mince words: "Improper guidance and feedback are the largest contributors to incompetence in the world of work."[1]

Gilbert stated unequivocally that employees need to know where the business is going. They also need *confirmation* of the contribution they make to business growth. Applying his ideas to real work situations, Gilbert concluded that by simply improving the communication of information to employees, performance could be improved by between 20 and 50 percent.[2]

From the mid-1980s, Gilbert's work helped spawn a range of new managerial behavioral approaches, including the concept of open-book management[3] and balanced scorecard.[4] The practical application of these new approaches, particularly open-book management (sharing financial information with all staff), has had varied success within organizations. For example, one feature of successful open-book management is the use of team-oriented decision-making meetings to increase understanding and drive business strategy. These meetings build the individual and collective commitment of employees by allowing them to be involved.

Too often, though, organizations are riveted on communicating information, believing that simply passing on facts and figures engages employees. Marketing specialist Kevin Thomson advocates applying the concepts of relationship marketing (see chapter 12) in these situations: "Treating employees as internal customers is the way forward. By using marketing-based communication strategies that match the needs of employees and create a two-way flow between the organization and its people, businesses can get far greater degrees of buy-in to corporate messages."[5]

In Thomson's assessment, even though technical tools have dramatically improved, the effectiveness of employee communications is actually worsening—and with significant consequences. A University of Salford (UK) study states that a majority of surveyed organizations score just 5.6 out of 10 for their effectiveness of communication. A U.S. Council of Communication Management study concludes that 64 percent of staff often do not believe their senior managers. Market and Opinion Research International further states that fewer than 50 percent of employees know their company's objectives.[6] Thomson concludes by saying, "If organizations buy in to the need for improving their businesses through their people, then improving the methods and means to capturing hearts and minds must be a priority."[7]

Internal brand marketing is one of the most powerful levers that can be used to support culture change, build internal alignment with the brand, and create enthusiasm for its delivery. Employees are no different from customers in that their needs are both emotional and logical. It seems glaringly obvious that similar principles and strategies can be applied to both sets of stakeholders. To engage employees, organizations must capture their imagination and commitment to the brand. Then and only then will they become internal brand loyalists and powerful external advocates of the brand promise.[8]

Seven guidelines for managing your internal brand communication

Many techniques can be used for effective communication. However, a number of specific guidelines apply when communicating internally about a brand.

1. *Communicate from your audience's point of view.* Internal brand communication must relate to employee issues, concerns, and aspirations about the brand. Staff desperately want to know what their work means to them, and they respond best when their views have been heard and understood. Before the executive team of Vodafone New Zealand (see previous chapter) embarked on a comprehensive communication process to engage staff in the brand and culture, the team members tested their messages with a group composed of staff relatives. Vodafone executives reckoned that if brand messages made sense to and inspired husbands, wives, and so on, they would do the same for staff.

2. *Connect with the heart as well as the head.* Thomas Gilbert once said, "we live in stories not statistics,"[9] yet so much of corporate language is lifeless and sterile. Hard messages are so much more

powerful and motivating if they are enveloped with emotion that reflects the brand. The key is not to focus solely upon information. Relationship marketing is about breadth and depth of communication, so you need to develop a range of communication styles that will connect with different types of people within an organization.

For example, TMI New Zealand created a cartoon character, AJ, to act as the brand champion to support an internal change process that was aimed at embedding a new brand position (business adrenalin) within a client's internal culture. AJ, short for Adrenalin Junkie, was the epitome of the brand values in action. At breakneck speed, AJ constantly reinforced the key messages, applauded the progress of an on-brand organization, and quietly challenged examples of off-brand behavior. AJ had a special newsletter, intranet page, and even his own e-mail address and phone number. He regularly "called" staff and customers to gather feedback. This proved to be highly effective because AJ brought a unique style of visibility that was both memorable and engaging.

3. *Use electronic communication as a complement rather than a substitute for in-person meetings.* Intranets can be great communication media for detailed information that staff must have. Similarly, e-mail has revolutionized our ability to communicate quickly and efficiently. However, in general, electronic media, including intranets and e-mail, are less effective because they are indirect and devoid of nonverbal cues. They fail to capture the emotional dimensions required for effective internal brand marketing.

4. *Be proactive in communication. It is said that nature abhors a vacuum.* This is also true about employee communication. When staff are not told what is happening, they will make up a reality as they talk with each other. Communication is especially critical during times of significant change, such as during mergers, or when a company

is trying to build a connection to its brand. Even if everything has been said before, new and interesting ways need to be found to support key brand messages. Take charge by profiling examples of on-brand behavior. Promote far-out ideas to spark alignment between the brand and service. Share strong feedback about customers' experiences. It's also all right to repeat your communication; in fact, this can be highly effective. Americans have heard the national anthem more than once, and many still get teary when it is sung well.

5. *Use the grapevine.* Because staff are often more likely to trust their peers, the company grapevine is a distinctly powerful tool. All too often managers either neglect it or react only when they hear misleading rumors. Smart organizations not only acknowledge that the grapevine exists, but they also harness its power by identifying key employees who influence it and then ensure these people are champions for brand messages.

6. *Focus on communication outcomes, not quantity of inputs.* In employee surveys, staff are often asked, "Do you feel you receive enough communication?" Almost inevitably, the response is no. The solution, however, is not more volume but rather more effective communication. Some organizations measure the quantity of internal communication—the number of newsletters, e-mails, and presentations to staff. Rather, managers need to inquire about every piece of communication: What was its impact? Did it support the desired outcome? Was it understood by all, and what did staff do differently because of it?

All too often managers assume that because they have sent out a message, it was heard. In fact, we have worked with dozens of companies where many staff outside the corporate office either never read the newsletters, memos, and e-mails in question or simply do not grasp what they were all about if they do read them.

7. *Remember that communication is a multidimensional process.* Many organizations operate from the premise that internal communication is about telling employees what is going on. However, today's workers have moved well beyond this paradigm. They seek an environment in which they can make a genuine contribution. Consequently, a company's internal communication strategy needs to ensure that it creates an exchange, not only between the management and staff but also among different staff groups. By giving staff regular opportunities to have their say, a means is developed to check and refine their understanding. It's the same principle as finding out what your customers are thinking and feeling. Face-to-face communication, preferably in small groups or one-on-one has the greatest impact on building consistency in interpretation and commitment.

Brand copy strategy

Written communications also strongly influence perceptions and beliefs. Consequently, identifying appropriate brand language to be used across all company communication media is necessary to embed the brand into the hearts and minds of staff.

Many organizations have detailed visual guidelines for their brands, including strict rules around how a brand can be represented and used in marketing literature, signage, and advertisements. However, very few have developed similar guidelines in relation to written words that relate to the brand. They do not have a brand copy strategy.

Brand thinker Mark Di Somma has a particular interest in the language of brands. He says it is not necessarily about conforming to a specific set of words but about ensuring that the spirit of the brand is always reflected when communication occurs. What you say orally is not the same as what you might write in a newsletter. However, all forms of communication should be accountable to and consistent with the brand. In Di Somma's words, "The power of a copy strategy is that it interprets the brand and sets rules for its expression. . . . As a result, every expression of the brand . . . adds to the dimension and character of the branded vernacular overall."[10]

A brand copy strategy offers the following benefits:

- It focuses on developing a consistent application of the brand essence in all written communication, be it press releases, Web pages, customer communication, or internal memos.
- It defines how the brand is reflected in external communication.
- It strongly influences the language and style of communication adopted inside the company.
- It has a powerful effect in reinforcing brands and key messages.

Writer's workshop

Once brand copy guidelines have been shaped and developed, they need to be adopted and applied throughout the organization. Di Somma says that selling the concept of a copy strategy at the organizational level is not always easy. Many initially struggle to see the relevance and impact. "It is one of those things that creeps up on them, but once it is embedded, they wonder how they ever appraised anything without it. One day, they find themselves intuitively responding not just to the words but to the spirit that those words or ideas represent."[11]

A writer's workshop is a powerful means to achieve consistent written communication. Such a workshop brings together managers and staff (including marketing, communications, and HR managers) whose primary responsibility is overseeing or producing various types of written communication. They are then offered a practical, and almost always needed and deeply appreciated, session in writing brand copy.

We recommend that the writer's workshop focus on at least two objectives: first, to help people develop a deeper understanding of the brand through immersion in the spirit of the brand and the underlying

off-brand

For many years, American Express told customers in television commercials that they were "always more than a number." In this world of multiple identity numbers, this is a refreshing position. Unfortunately, the first thing customers saw on almost every piece of written correspondence was their card number. And when customers rang the AmEx call centers, what do you think was the first thing asked of them?

brand values; and second, to teach practical skills in how to write in an on-brand manner. It is advisable that the practical exercises offered in the workshop start with easy examples, such as how to write a direct marketing brochure for a service you offer. Then move toward more difficult examples, such as how to write a letter responding to a complaint in an on-brand manner or how, in an on-brand fashion, to say no to a customer.

When it is done well, a copy strategy gives everyone a powerful framework from which to work. In addition, it provides a standard against which to judge all the written work your organization produces. Your brand style will become infused in all your communications—both external and internal—creating consistency in your brand messages.

The outside in: your external marketing impacts your insides

After Neil Armstrong stepped on the moon, someone at NASA commented that NASA had a significant advantage in achieving a very difficult goal: every night the engineers could actually see their goal. Constantly seeing your brand also plays a powerful role in aligning culture and service with the brand. Every advertisement, billboard, brochure, and sign can remind staff of their brand promise and, assuming they have been exposed to branded customer service concepts, their role in delivering on-brand service.

Organizations that successfully brand their customer service grasp that advertising is designed as much for employees as it is for customers. The brand and the story communicated in advertising highlight staff spirit, attitude, and values. Unfortunately, this opportunity is frequently lost, especially when advertising is used primarily to promote specific products or offerings. Even worse, sometimes advertising undermines the branded customer service proposition.

Recently a large division of a major commercial bank asked TMI to review the alignment between its new brand positioning ("100 Percent Professional Care") and its service culture. Management successfully sold the brand to staff by reinforcing the critical role they played in delivering the brand promise through high-quality customer service. The "100 Percent Professional Care" promise was launched to staff at a big, splashy event. Employees loved the idea and were excited about the personal role they were asked to play in supporting the brand.

A few months later, a low-budget advertising campaign was launched with the goal of attracting new customers and building awareness of this division. When public awareness measurably increased, marketers believed they were successful. But the experience was deflating for the staff. In discussion after discussion, we heard one consistent lament: "The look and feel of the advertising doesn't reflect our promise of 100 Percent Professional Care." The ads were off-brand!

Many staff lost their sense of aspiration about the brand, and their motivation to deliver it was diminished. A single advertisement set an expectation of service that certainly did not require staff to stretch. It actually implied they were overdelivering on service.

8

Internal Word of Mouth: The Role of Brand Champions

It is estimated that up to 75 percent of organizational change processes fail because of people issues. Designing a change process to brand customer service is a relatively contained process. Implementing it is long-term and ongoing. We have learned that keeping everyone interested and engaged over the long haul is at the heart of the issue to avoid failure.

While support from upper management is obviously critical, it can be seductive to understate the role that general staff play in the brand integration process. And there is no better way to jump-start this engagement than with brand champions.

The role of brand champions

The brand champion process operates much the same way that marketing professionals gain public exposure. Both aim for critical masses of people thinking of their brand first. Branded customer service is not likely to be consistently delivered if employees feel they are forced to comply with on-brand behavioral standards (push projects). It takes time and resources to create commitment (pull) for delivering on-brand service, but it is an investment that will reduce catch-up efforts demanded down the road to remove employee resistance.

Think of brand champions as internal sponsors for your branded customer service initiatives. As figure 5 indicates, brand champions can cascade sponsorship for your brand throughout your entire business, influencing behavior on a daily basis.

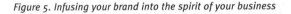

Figure 5. Infusing your brand into the spirit of your business

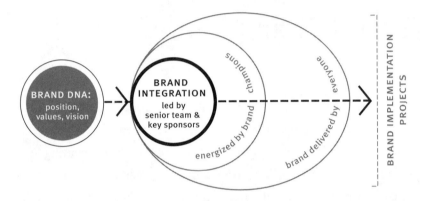

One of the striking benefits of working with a brand champion team is that it is easily monitored to provide a quick measurement of how far on-brand behaviors have penetrated the organization. If the brand champions do not deliver the brand promise in their behaviors, chances are that the rest of the organization is not delivering. They reflect what is happening with your entire internal branding effort.

Brand champions, as table 4 indicates, can play a variety of roles. Here are the three most critical:

1. *Live the brand.* Keep the branded customer service orientation alive and visible through demonstrable behavior.

2. *Support and advance the vision.* Implement and measure the impact of as many good ideas as possible to support branded customer service efforts.

3. *Work as one team.* Act as internal consultants and inspire the entire organization; become a resource to senior management.

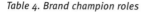

Table 4. Brand champion roles

LIVE THE BRAND	SUPPORT AND ADVANCE THE VISION	WORK AS ONE TEAM
• Share their understanding of the brand • Push an ideal picture of the brand • Practice brand values	• Help plan and implement the vision • Measure progress • Coordinate implementation	• Exchange brand information • Coordinate brand communication • Host update meetings

Walk into a Krispy Kreme Doughnuts location and you will find animated staff who are excited about being part of a successful corporation. They are proud of their product, which brings smiles to their customers' mouths. Krispy Kreme's product, if consumed in large amounts, will make you obese. Doughnuts aren't that good for your energy level—or your teeth. Yet tremendous levels of enthusiasm are evident in the Krispy Kreme outlets. In contrast, we have visited large pharmaceutical companies engaged in the production and distribution of drugs that save lives but having none of Krispy Kreme's enthusiasm.

One of the big differences is that Krispy Kreme early on paid attention to commitment; the outlet managers are, in effect, the brand champions for the huge doughnut maker. Conversely, many older corporations didn't begin their enterprises paying attention to staff mood, customer focus issues, and branding. To expect managers in such corporations to suddenly assume the role of brand champions is wishful thinking. A brand champion team composed of staff members who are genuinely excited about what they do has a much better chance of fulfilling the three major roles required of brand champions.

Whom to nominate as brand champions

Brand champion teams are best composed of between two and twenty cross-functional and multilevel members. If your business is widely dispersed, you need at least two brand champions at each location. This way you will have a "spare" if one leaves. Brand championing can become a lonely affair at times, and the brand supporters need support themselves!

It is possible to nominate one brand champion for each department. However, we have not seen this work as effectively as identifying a cross-functional team. When brand champions are identified with a department, they begin to feel the burden of this responsibility as extra work. They also tend to remain more committed to their department than to the brand champion team. A group of brand champions working together and not representing departments, however, is extremely different.

Choosing the members of this team can be a sensitive issue because being nominated is generally considered desirable. Sometimes managers know which staff are natural leaders. In larger organizations, division managers may get so many volunteers that they will need to conduct interviews to make the right choice.

Choose your brand champions based on what is required of them. Behavioral requirements are a good standard for selection. Here is a possible beginning checklist of requirements:

- Being the driving force for the branded service promise by sharing energy, enthusiasm, and knowledge
- Living the vision—i.e., leading by example
- Getting things done
- Acting as networkers, catalysts, and peacemakers
- Becoming cheerleaders, inspiring and exciting people and what they do

- Being unofficial listening points for other staff
- Respecting people's confidences
- Creating internal public relations for who you are and what you do

We are frequently asked if high-level managers should serve on brand champion teams. In most cases, we do not recommend this. A manager who meets the same requirements as the brand champions (see the list above) can be an adviser or consultant to the group. Obviously, someone needs to take responsibility for the brand champions, and a well-positioned adviser can fulfill this function.

However, when strong-willed managers have been included on these teams, we have seen employees immediately defer to the manager, which stifles staff creativity. We know of a brand champion team led by a general manager. Not surprisingly, that group got a great deal done, but nothing was initiated by the team. A brand champion team needs to take responsibility for originating, organizing, and completing tasks, rather than merely fulfilling tasks assigned by management.

For this reason, we also recommend that the initial team building be facilitated by someone from outside the firm. If this is not done, the dynamics of the organization can be so strong that the brand champions will tend to fall in line with perceived management requirements. Any facilitator who is an employee of the organization will be seen as a mouthpiece for management imperatives. A facilitator from outside the organization will be better able to craft a dynamic whereby the team takes responsibility for itself and its carefully defined role.

Clients we have worked with have benefited from their brand champions in different ways. One, for example, assigned its brand champions the task of running brand induction programs. In that case, the champions had to be skilled facilitators, comfortable working with groups. In other instances, the brand champions became spokespeople for the organization in marketing efforts. In those cases, the champions had to be effective when in front of the media.

TMI has also worked with clients where TMI consultants delivered the brand induction messages. In these cases, the brand champions became the host team for those meetings. This is a great experience for them. They get to meet a large part of the organization, they effectively learn the messages of the branded customer service program, they develop meeting management skills, and they remove a significant burden from human resources staff to handle the details of program logistics.

Normally, brand champions continue their regular jobs. If the work of championing on-brand service is significant, and it can be, then brand champions need to have authority to devote a percentage of their time to this activity. Because of time demands, brand champions should rotate on and off the team. This not only gives fresh blood and ideas to the team, but it also creates a definitive time frame for service. Brand championing can take a substantial amount of time, depending upon the energy of the team, and members need to know they will not be obligated forever. A rotating membership is probably best with six-month-long rotations and with tenures no longer than one and a half to two years. To start a rotating membership, one-third of the group would serve just one six-month rotation, another third would serve two rotations, and the final third would serve the full one and a half years. Thereafter, every group would serve three six-month rotations, with one-third of the members being replaced every six months.

Education for brand champions

If there ever was a need for team building with an organized group, it is with brand champions. They need to get to know each other and identify special talents of the team members. Then when tough tasks must be accomplished, the team will already know its strengths and be able to move ahead. By understanding its weaknesses, the team will also know when to seek outside help.

Brand champions also need time to communicate with each other. We recommend the following communication vehicles for the team to stay in regular contact:

- Five-minute debriefing at the beginning of each day to verbally inform each other about highlights of the previous day. If the team members are located at different sites, they need to regularly check in by teleconference or videoconference.
- A message board in the brand champion office to track events, monitor task accomplishments, and pose questions. The team needs its own space to establish its unique identity.
- A regular time for scheduled meetings.
- Longer periods of time for strategic planning. A good time for this is when the team changes membership, once every six months.

We have found that most brand champions need development in the areas of

- choosing and managing projects
- learning how to give constructive criticism in a positive style
- communicating so they can sell their ideas to colleagues
- turning discussions with colleagues into open-ended conversations
- using questions to bridge conflicts
- listening empathically
- handling disagreements

Brand champions, if chosen well, can be an exceptionally high-energy group. They may tend to take on too many initiatives, not realizing they have to make choices. Utilizing a decision matrix like table 5 can help them make better choices, particularly when they begin this process. They can evaluate every project according to the five criteria listed so they choose projects that are reasonable but have high impact.

Table 5. Decision matrix

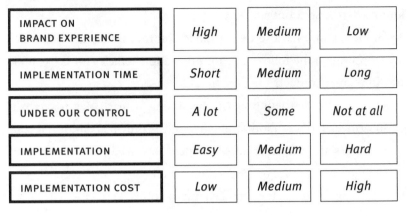

IMPACT ON BRAND EXPERIENCE	High	Medium	Low
IMPLEMENTATION TIME	Short	Medium	Long
UNDER OUR CONTROL	A lot	Some	Not at all
IMPLEMENTATION	Easy	Medium	Hard
IMPLEMENTATION COST	Low	Medium	High

The ideas that a brand champion team can implement are literally endless. When company-wide brand induction programs are organized, we recommend asking participants to write letters outlining changes they think need to be made in order for them to fully implement on-brand service. Astounding ideas come from such letters. After all, many of these ideas are from people who are fully immersed in customer contact. When people sign their names to their letters, we encourage the brand champions to personally respond to these individuals within forty-eight hours to thank them for their input. It is astonishing what these letters can do to ignite an organization, especially when staff see that something is being done with their input.

Management support for brand champions

When the brand champions are well integrated in an organization, the team becomes highly visible. This group needs to be treated as special but without elevating it to a position where members are held in disdain by the rest of the staff. (That would be highly counterproductive!) It requires a delicate balancing act of using the talents of such a high-energy group while not creating animosity or jealousy about its existence.

Brand champions must not be set up to fail, so their beginning efforts need to be positive and look good to the rest of the organization. They normally need help with this in the form of a brand toolbox that includes guidelines, suggested activities they can implement, access to organizational leadership, and even a budget.

Finally, the position of the brand champion team needs to be viewed positively by senior management. Making sure the team is well supported at the highest levels of the organization will help enormously. You clearly do not want a situation where your brand champions are spreading the word that this is a process only on paper and not being lived and supported by management.

For this reason, the idea of brand champions has to be sold to senior managers first. They need to know what this group of people will be doing. Situations must be anticipated where toes may be stepped on. A brand champion team needs to have the ability to move throughout the entire organization, and a single manager who opposes the team's efforts can weaken the entire process.

We once led a process that involved upwards of twenty brand champions. They were an extremely engaged group. People fought to get onto the first team. Everyone on the team exemplified the values of the brand; we were assured of this because of our involvement in selecting the team members. A three-day team-building process began the team's integration. We planned a special opening in a darkened room with music, rich graphics, and a themed *Mission Impossible* ("Should you decide to accept this mission . . .") introduction of all the team members. By the time we finished with the introduction, all the participants were on their feet, clapping and shouting—clearly involved with the process!

At this point the managing director came into the room to offer a welcome to the team. Normally, he was fairly upbeat, but he had had a bad morning and was under considerable budgetary stress—at least, these were the only explanations we could find for his completely off-brand behavior. He walked to the front of the room and opened his remarks with a dash of cold water: "This isn't about fun. This is about hard work."

Actually, one of the organization's brand values did involve fun, so the remarks particularly stung the group. It took a lot of skill on the part of the facilitator to handle this issue so that the director's welcome to the team members did not become their reality. Fortunately, that did not happen, though we often wonder how much better this team might have performed if it had had a different welcome.

Brand champions as monitors of on- and off-brand behavior

All customers have no doubt heard service representatives berate their colleagues for something they have or haven't done. Every time we overhear this type of dialogue, we can very easily imagine ourselves as customers paying the price for the behavior being discussed. For example, we heard a car repair shop receptionist complain to her colleague, "They never answer the phone back there," and we assumed that probably was why our call wasn't answered earlier in the day.

Brand champions can do a great deal to mitigate the impact of this type of chatter that very frequently takes place in front of customers. First, they can listen to it, and second, they can initiate steps to remedy the problem.

Think about the receptionist complaining to her colleague about the back-office staff never answering the phone. They both needed someone to listen to their complaint. They could either go directly to the back-office staff to tell them the consequences of their behavior or go to someone who could involve the appropriate manager. This "someone" can be a brand champion, who either would talk with the back-office staff or ask for managerial assistance.

For this reason, HR managers need to stay closely connected to the brand champions. Because brand champions hold their regular jobs, as well as being brand champions, they may hear about situations through the staff grapevine that someone in HR may not. Brand champions, in effect, can become staff that do not work in HR but who can spread the reach of critical HR functions. They, therefore, also need highly developed interpersonal skills to handle delicate situations, such as one employee complaining about another.

It is easy to see how this type of simple event can become very complicated if the brand champions' scope of activity and power to act are not carefully decided in advance. When not sensitively positioned, the brand champions can be seen as brand champion police—not a good thing.

It is possible to put too heavy of a burden on a brand champion team. For example, if you expect them to be the major communication channel for all internal messages about your brand, the brand champions will become too instrumental in the process, no doubt exceeding their communication capacity. The brand champions play a better role as reinforcers. They do not start the party, but they make sure it continues.

Brand champions as connectors

Malcolm Gladwell in *The Tipping Point* looks at how social movements take root and become widespread. His work is based on principles that explain how infections become contagious. Gladwell labels this contagious atmosphere as the Tipping Point, that point where behavior is no longer sporadic but quickly and fully penetrates a system.[1]

Gladwell suggests that part of what pushes an idea over this point to become a trend is that it is led by "connectors." Ed Keller and Jon Berry refer to them as the "influentials" in their book by the same title. Keller and Berry argue that the influentials are more important today than ever before because of the fragmented market that advertisers now encounter.[2]

Connectors or influentials are people who know a lot of other people from a wide variety of groups. Obviously, these trendsetters who try out new ideas and new products make great brand champions. In large organizations, connectors can sometimes be found in departments such as shipping or other business services because they typically know everyone. Frequently they are gregarious and extroverted, though not necessarily. One thing is for certain, they generally possess one characteristic in boundless amounts: the desire to share information. As Gladwell writes, "[T]here are exceptional people out there who are capable of starting epidemics. All you have to do is find them."[3]

Those people are your brand champions. Your task is to identify them and support them to continue the ongoing work of making the message of branded customer service "sticky," another of Gladwell's change factors. Stickiness is a way of presenting ideas so they are memorable and accomplish their purpose. Again, in Gladwell's words, "There is a simple way to package information that, under the right circumstances, can make it irresistible. All you have to do is to find it."[4]

Our experience tells us that if you make connectors or influentials your internal brand champions, they have a better chance of creating these sticky messages. Natural leaders from across the organization tend to know how to sell ideas in an irresistible manner. If your brand isn't irresistible, then you need to go back to the drawing board and look at your brand DNA.

You also need help from your human resources department.

9

Human Resources: The Window to the Corporate Soul

Human resource departments are undergoing a profound change. Since the advent of the balanced scorecard concept,[1] organizations around the world have begun to position their human capital expertise as one of the strategic elements of business success. While some HR departments are still primarily filling out forms, handling staff benefit issues, and making sure the organization is in compliance with labor laws, growing numbers of HR professionals have become strategic consultants to top management. In fact, software now makes it possible for line managers in many organizations to handle a lot of traditional HR administration, leaving HR time to focus on organizational development and human performance. And many HR departments no longer handle training, now a separate department in many large organizations.

Dr. Graeme Field, an organizational development principal with Morgan and Banks (NZ), explains that when organizations understand that people are its competitive edge, the HR role "includes devising recruitment policy and strategy to ensure an organization hires people that fit its culture and value its customers . . . [and] be able to formulate methods to accurately measure individual employee and overall staff performance."[2] Critical in this role is also balancing the needs of investors, employees, and customers. To emphasize this new positioning, some recommend calling HR departments human capital departments. Whatever they are called, if an organization attempts to brand its customer service, HR must be brought into the marketing and branding process.

Staff recruitment

A strong brand is a powerful draw for recruitment. It is also a pull to retain valued staff. In order for an organization to be seen as a desirable place to work, HR must first hire people who can live and deliver the brand. No longer can "warm bodies," as some managers call them, be recruited to fill service positions. This requires both identifying competencies and also defining the type of person who will best deliver the brand's promise. Not so long ago, the big challenge was hiring staff that could handle technological changes. Today, that challenge may be brand delivery competence.

Abercrombie and Fitch (A&F) has taken this idea to an extreme. The big clothing retailer actively recruits young college students who look like its catalog models. Such a person is at least good-looking and young and frequently has what is described as a distinctive classic American look. We heard someone describe A&F staff as surfers who just caught a wave. According to the *New York Times*, the clothing retailer, in its hiring approach, is merely part of a growing retail hiring trend.[3]

Abercrombie and Fitch knows well that young shoppers prefer coming into stores to be waited on by staff who look and act like its ads. The question is whether A&F violates antidiscrimination laws by hiring within such a narrow range. Hiring for looks is not necessarily illegal, but not hiring because of age, sex, or ethnicity is.

Should a company that wants to project youth and energy in its brand be allowed to fire workers after they reach a certain age or never hire them in the first place? Marshall Cohen, senior industry analyst with NPD Fashion World, argues, "In today's competitive retail environment, the methods have changed for capturing the consumers' awareness of your brand. Being able to find a brand enhancer, or what I call a walking billboard, is critical."[4]

Certainly, education and skill are considered fair measures for hiring. And no one seems to object that high-fashion models are almost all very tall, skinny, and beautiful, or at least exotic. But what about the case of Abercrombie and Fitch? Some individuals have brought legal complaints (A&F is currently facing two high-profile racial discrimination cases) stating that they were turned down for jobs, even though they brought substantial retail experience with them. Instead, good-looking young people without any retail experience have been recruited. A clue as to A&F's mind-set is that A&F apparently does not place a great emphasis on service training. We have asked several stunning-looking A&F clerks about the training they received and were told they got a two-hour orientation. Clearly, if Abercrombie and Fitch can openly recruit this way, it gains an advantage over other retailers that hire older experienced shop clerks who look like the parents or grandparents of the audience they wish to attract.

Actually, A&F has recently discovered that attractive sales staff are not enough to command market share if its target market is too narrow. A&F has made its brand so exclusionary that same-store sales have dropped for four years in a row.[5] Brands are a total package and obviously involve more than the physical appearance of sales clerks.

To hire for effective branded service delivery, HR must first define the brand delivery skills necessary for each position. HR professionals can do it themselves or work with managers to describe brand requirements that go beyond detailing technical skills and task responsibilities. Then, just as references and background information need to be checked and skills need to be tested, so, too, do brand delivery approaches need to be assessed. If your organization has a probationary period before permanent hiring, attitudes toward the brand need to be considered part of the final hiring decision.

Some brand delivery attitudes can be taught—to a point. For example, Intel's brand promises speed. Intel can educate staff about how to deliver the concept of speed in service delivery, but someone who habitually speaks and reacts slowly is probably not the best person to work at an Intel call center. FedEx is about guarantees ("When it positively, absolutely has to be there overnight"). FedEx needs to consider what a "guaranteed delivery" service attitude looks and sounds like, as opposed to what a "probably there on time but cheaper" package service attitude looks and sounds like.

Discussing the tone that is required with potential employees, and reminding them of it during their tenure, makes it more likely that employees will be alerted to its significance and what is expected of them. When offering suggestions for performance improvement, managers need to do so in terms of the brand. This helps to depersonalize criticism, making it easier to accept. For example, if reliability and personal organization are aspects of your brand promise, then suggestions for keeping a more organized desk can be framed within brand delivery and not around how messy the person is.

For many years, TMI has recommended writing job descriptions from the customers' point of view. We have discovered that this approach can be readily shifted to focus on brands. Most job descriptions are written from the point of view of what the employee does. But in a customer-centric organization, how customers benefit from what employees do is a better starting point for a job description. In a brand-centric organization, including an element of the brand promise brings more precise definition to the essential brand aspects of a position.

For example, ARAMARK Uniform Services designs, manufactures, and cleans work uniforms. From its customers' point of view, however, it "gives people a corporate identity." From a brand point of view with service identified as ARAMARK's competitive differentiator, the description becomes "We make it possible for customers to have complete confidence in their visible corporate identity." Then the task becomes to identify potential staff who identify with and can support such a brand promise whether they are designing, manufacturing, or cleaning uniforms.

On-brand hiring practices: Pret a Manger

Visit the Pret a Manger Web site (http://www.pretamanger.com) and you will immediately understand Pret's brand promise in words printed white on red and exuding passion—passion, passion about food. Passion about everything the company does.

The UK-based Pret, founded in 1986, is described by the *London Times* as having "revolutionized the concept of sandwich making and eating."[6] A big part of Pret's success has to do with its staff. Pret hires only about 5 percent of those who apply for a position. Possible recruits are interviewed multiple times and are finally given a "test day" in a Pret shop. Shop employees finally decide who gets hired.

Again in Pret's words: "We are equally passionate about the people we employ. We're incredibly privileged that so many creative, hard working and talented people have chosen to work for us. . . . We employ people with personality who we think have the potential to give genuinely good service—people who like mixing with other people, who are good-humored and like to enjoy themselves."[7]

If hiring is done well and you have a critical mass of employees who are engaged with the brand, off-brand staff will feel uncomfortable working with you. They will be misfits; their service delivery approaches and attitudes will not be tolerated by the on-brand staff.

Brand book

Every organization also needs a blueprint or Brand Book to guide its branded customer service effort. The Brand Book is best made with joint input from the marketing and HR departments. Vendors and outside agencies should look at the final product to give feedback about its contents. They may notice disparities or conflicts that are hard to see from the inside.

We recommend a high-quality, colorful, and engaging publication that is representative of your brand promise. It should minimally contain the following:

- A welcome from the senior person in your organization
- Mission statement
- Vision statement
- Company information
- Brand goals and strategy
- Brand promise and values
- Brand history information
- Brand differentiators
- Branded customer service practices

Some organizations also include personnel and orientation materials in Brand Books: organizational structure, locations, products, names of key players, and departments. Others include information about dress codes, appearance, benefits, guidelines for employee behavior, recognition programs, and commonly asked questions and their answers.

All this is possible. Think about the Brand Book as a marketing document for your staff. And be aware that copies of it will no doubt circulate to the general public, news media, and your competitors. Every Brand Book we have been involved with has been interesting to read and visually appealing. It is important that this corporate document not be another three-ring binder that gets put on a shelf and never looked at again. It should be compelling enough so people refer to it when in meetings, when making important strategic decisions, and when they have a question about what their organization is doing. An effective Brand Book is a guide to your brand DNA.

Brand study: the role of HR at the Isle of Capri Casinos

TMI has had the opportunity to work with the Isle of Capri Casinos, the world's seventh largest casino, over an extended period. The Isle provides a complete example of what can happen when HR is invited to play a strategic role in developing a brand and a business.[8]

Predominantly a riverboat casino in smaller (compared to Las Vegas and Atlantic City) gaming markets, the Isle spearheaded the development of the Mississippi Gulf as a gaming destination. When the Isle first invited TMI to work with its staff, it had just acquired the Lady Luck casinos, doubling its size. The Isle requested help with two challenges: to spark a branded style of customer service that would be delivered consistently throughout all its properties and to emphasize a distinct Isle of Capri culture across all the newly acquired properties. What were the overall results? Problems stemming from the merger issues immediately and fundamentally disappeared. Significant progress has been made on branding the Isle's customer service.

The first stage of TMI's work involved establishing a baseline with an audit. Today, the HR department continues to gather metrics across a wide range of activities in the Isle's attempt to become a "top box" company—that is, a desired place to work as well as a home to its guests.

Management briefings were first facilitated at the corporate and senior management level and then moved to all the Isle properties. This assured that Isle property managers understood what was happening and let them know how they were critical in supporting this process. Internal brand champions, called Navigation Teams, were organized. These teams played host for the two-day branded customer service intervention that twelve thousand Isle team members attended. Programs were held in a tightly concentrated three-month period with sessions offered across all three shifts of the twenty-four-hour operation. Isle corporate leaders personally either opened or closed over 90 percent of these programs. The idea behind concentrating the brand communication effort was to dramatically shift the organization in the shortest time possible.

The Isle's mission had already been defined: not the biggest but the best—best for its guests, best for its employees, best for its communities, and best for its investors. The Isle's HR vision is to be "a best place to work," to operate as an employer of choice. This HR vision is tied to the Isle's overall service delivery, which the employees aspire to living internally as much as they deliver it to their guests. Every year, the executive team establishes five strategic goals that relate to aspects of this mission. Action plans and budgets are established to accomplish these goals as actions cascade down at a furious pace through the organization.

The Isle also had defined its brand of service. On a rational level the Isle's brand is "Each Isle of Capri facility offers comprehensive and satisfying entertainment, dining, shopping, and a variety of special events." On an emotional level, the brand is "CAPRI (Courteous, Attentive, Playful, Resourceful, and Impassioned)." Its brand promise is "Isle Style means fun." Fun means playful, courteous, impassioned, and reasonably priced, and guests are known by name. The Isle's logo is a picture of a macaw perched on the letters of the "Isle of Capri Casino." The bird is an important part of the Isle's identification. At all the Isle properties, you will find exotic, live macaws, all playfully named Eno.

The challenges the Isle faces are twofold: managing high staff turnover, which is common in the hospitality industry, and making sure its management style is in harmony with its brand elements. Isle managers are highly committed to this process; they understand it is not a simple one. They work with simultaneous multiple interventions. Every time we interact with the sprawling Isle organization, we are again reminded of Jim Collins's statement that we quoted earlier about "a giant heavy flywheel, turn upon turn, building momentum until breakthrough, and beyond."[9]

After completing the first wave of branded service programs, Isle executives invited TMI to return to the properties with a series of eight half-day management and supervisory programs for its seventeen hundred managers and supervisors.[10] As a part of these programs, each management topic was looked at through the lens of "CAPRI" brand delivery. One of the courses was about staff retention. After considering the human and financial costs of high staff turnover and what to do about it, we looked at what would be involved in retaining team members while delivering CAPRI branded service. Questions were posed that related to each of the brand attributes, for example: A: How can you be *attentive* so team members feel they are special every day they come to the Isle? and I: How can you be *impassioned* about your team members as part of your strategy to retain them?

A series of on-brand and off-brand behaviors were suggested that related to each management topic. On-brand leadership, for example, involved

- communicating the Isle vision clearly and consistently
- delivering focused service messages while communicating with team members
- being willing to display passion about the Isle and its products

Off-brand leadership meant

- assuming that team members know and understand the Isle's vision
- judging staff as stupid if they don't buy in to the Isle vision
- Assuming that team members will be motivated if they merely focus on the functions of their jobs

A group of Isle leaders also identified functional areas of the Isle and then listed all customer touch points in each of these areas that could be looked at through the eyes of the CAPRI brand. These touch points were brainstormed to find ways that they could be delivered CAPRI style: Courteous, Attentive, Playful, Resourceful, and Impassioned. By the end of this session, the potentiality of defining the Isle's culture with the brand was more than apparent.

TMI was then asked to help the Isle of Capri in a half-day empowerment program called The Power to Please. During this process, a forty-one-page Brand Book was produced that continues to be distributed to all Isle team members. The Isle has since set up a mentoring program, it gathers metrics, it is assessing the efficacy of its training programs, and it continues to work with all incoming staff to see that they are imbued with the Isle culture.

Will this continue? Nothing is guaranteed, of course, but we believe it will for two reasons. First, the executive team members are strongly committed to being the best in their markets. They understand achieving this goal is not a one-COO process. They have transitioned from one COO to the next, and their brand efforts continue under Tim Hinkley's leadership. Robert Boone, corporate vice president for HR, plays a strategic role in deciding the direction of the Isle. Isle managers all understand that gaming customers have many other choices, but they are committed to positioning the Isle of Capri with its service so when a customer thinks "fun," the Isle comes to mind first. Second, the Isle's culture is strongly blended with its external branding. We hear it in the employees' conversations with us; we see it when we visit the Isle's properties; we watch it in its corporate meetings.

Is the Isle there yet? No, but it is much closer than it was four years ago when we first met its managers. As of the writing of this book, the Isle has just announced *record* first quarter results. It is beginning to win awards for its internal functions; customer service experts write about it.

Its other statistics? When we first met Isle executives, staff turnover rates were at 60 percent. Today they are at 34 percent, and these are the lowest in the industry.[11] The Isle has had no difficulty filling staff positions when it opens in new markets. When it opened its casino in Boonville, Missouri, unemployment was less than 2.6 percent. The Isle attracted almost two thousand people who wanted to work for it— 90 percent of whom were already working for someone else.

Two questions that people frequently pose to companies that are successful with culture change efforts are, "Why are you sharing all this information? Isn't this your competitive advantage?" We believe that the organizations that engage in such a process understand their template is not their competitive advantage. It's just a road map. Implemented action is what counts. And this is action that has to be made on a detailed and daily basis. Remember, service is your brand in action.

We once heard the head of Harrah's Casinos speak to approximately 150 of his competitors at a Las Vegas gaming conference. He spelled out very clearly what Harrah's is doing that he believes contributes to its market growth. Someone in the audience raised his hand and asked, "Aren't you afraid of sharing all this information with us?" The CEO's answer was, "No. We know you guys won't do it anyway."

There's a certain amount of truth to this. We believe there is also a second reason. Even if you adopted Harrah's or the Isle of Capri's basic road map, you would still have to tailor the process and ideas to fit your business. If you just duplicated what the Isle of Capri or Harrah's is doing, you might be better than you currently are, but you would certainly not be a differentiated brand.

In order to create some of the magic going on at the Isle of Capri and Harrah's, you need your own brand toolbox.

Part III

The Branded Customer Service Toolbox

Once you have defined your brand DNA (see chapter 4), you need some tools to ensure your brand has the best chance of actually being delivered by your staff.

This part of the book provides you with dozens of sample exercises you can conduct with staff so your brand promise will be understood in a way that it will more likely be delivered. This part of the book also explores how your sales process can be integrated into the total brand delivery process.

In chapter 12, brand awareness exercises for staff are divided into four types:

1. Brand knowledge: What are brands all about?
2. Brand specificity: What is unique about our brand?
3. Brand assessment: Are we on-brand or off-brand?
4. Brand delivery: What does our brand look like in action?

Management brand support exercises are divided into three types:

1. Brand support for staff
2. Brand reinforcement communication
3. Brand alignment

The toolbox is completed with a series of exercises about selling in a branded world.

10

Great Brands Are Supported from Within: The Role of Management

Employment branding, that is, communicating the brand message to staff, is an idea that has gained momentum in recent years among branding experts. Brand expert Michael T. Ewing says,

> [Employment branding] may be due to the realization that advertising is probably the most visible, recognizable and memorable element of organizational communication. As such, it has the potential to become a purveyor of organizational symbolism and mythology and thus to be part of the cultural, ritual and interpretive organizational fabric that is the thick medium through which leadership creates climate and thus organized action.[1]

Imagine the type of organization to which Ewing could be referring. It would be well defined and repeatedly communicated to staff at both rational and emotional levels. Organizational purpose and values would be clear, relevant, and understood by everyone. In such a situation, employees would more likely live the values that underpin who they are and what they stand for as an organization. The brand, delivered with product quality, service delivery, advertising, product and service guarantees, history, and name, would become a focal point of organizational cultural communication. Imagine the focus, energy, and momentum for performance that could be created within such an environment!

Interest in employment branding has arisen as more people realize that the major responsibility for delivering the brand promise lies in staff's hands. For many organizations, however, staff buy-in to brand values is extremely limited. A survey of one hundred senior corporate executives from major European corporations revealed that only 36 percent thought that buy-in to brand mission, vision, and values went further than senior management. The reasons cited for these weak numbers included a failure to communicate what the brand stands for because of fragmentation, weaknesses in internal communication channels, lack of clarity in the brand, decentralization, and failure to spell out brand relevance to employees.[2]

U.S.-based Kemper Insurance Company is an organization where key executives are interested in everyone at Kemper understanding the brand. When they were asked what they wanted to accomplish with a recent advertising campaign, executives said it was primarily to advertise core values (responsibility, quality, and integrity) to its agents, brokers, and employees.

Kemper found that humorous test ads had a high likability factor with audiences. The people who watched them, however, did not connect the funny ads to Kemper's brand identity and values. So Kemper decided to launch serious core-value commercials at a sponsored major golf tournament on CBS. After the campaign, Joel Borgardt, vice president of corporate marketing, concluded, "[The ad campaign has been] a good rallying point for the employees, and agents and brokers can relate to it as well. It's not about just an advertising campaign; it's about people living the values every day."[3] Kemper's president, Bill

Smith, emphasized this point by describing how the insurance giant linked its strategic business plan with branding: "A brand is a combination of a people's perceptions of a company and their experiences with it. The relationships we build at Kemper are a key driver of these perceptions and are the foundation of a strong brand."[4]

The brand or the bland: defining your brand in the mind of your staff

We have stated that branding is the sum of all the impressions customers form of the experiences they have with your brand. A less obvious conclusion, though equally important, is that branding is also the sum of experiences that staff have with the brand and the products they represent.

The staff-brand relationship is a special, multidimensional one that must be carefully nurtured, particularly when staff rarely or never use the product or sample the service they represent. This situation can happen because the product just happens to be one that staff would never use, such as farm tractors or large business software programs. It can also include products that are out of the price range of staff, such as expensive hotel rooms, luxury watches, or high-end automobiles.

We have stayed in hotels where the front desk clerks have never even been inside the guest rooms. With an almost total lack of knowledge of what a consumer experiences, it is difficult for staff to grasp what might enhance or detract from the brand. In these circumstances, staff can look at the situation *only* from their own perspective. They have no other context from which to understand what is happening to the consumer.

Years ago, Janelle and her family traveled throughout China on an extensive and lengthy trip. They each had two pieces of luggage, not an exorbitant number given the distance and length of their trip.

Wherever they went, hotel personnel, taxi drivers, and train conductors all clucked their tongues and said, "Xingli tai duo," or in English, "Too much luggage."

Admittedly, the luggage was bulging, but under the circumstances and given everything they bought on the trip, two pieces per person was definitely not "too much luggage." But how were the local staff to know what is involved with a lengthy international trip where every purchasable item looks exotic and exciting? Most Chinese in the early 1980s had little money and probably had not been out of their province, let alone taken a trip to the other side of the world.

We have urged hotel executives in developing nations to make sure all of the staff have the opportunity to stay overnight in one of the guest rooms. This taste of the brand is an important part of educating staff about the product they represent. But that is just the beginning for getting the touch and feel of your brand into the minds of your staff.

Some brand concepts are very complex, and simple knowledge possessed by staff of products or services will not be sufficient to impact customers with the brand. Research suggests that not only does full understanding of the organizational brand reduce employee stress, but it also increases the likelihood that staff will deliver the brand.[5]

This understanding can be difficult to achieve. The new brand position of Hallmark Entertainment Network (now owned by Crown Media International, for example, was developed so that "viewers can experience a sense of growth, have a better understanding of life and appreciate it all with new meaning,"[6] says Andrew Brilliant, Crown Media's executive deputy CEO. How do you get those ideas solidly placed in the receptionist's mind, for example, so he or she can reinforce this concept whenever anyone calls Hallmark? Brand learning experiences, such as those detailed in the brand toolbox, can start you on this road.

The value of repeated communications

In order to live its promise of the "Love Airline," Southwest puts a high priority on hiring attitudes when recruiting. The airline, therefore, reiterates its values every time it hires someone. In its recruitment process, for example, prospective employees are likely to be tested for their ability to make fun of themselves. To measure altruism, a typical interview question might be to recall a moment when they felt proud about something they did. If candidates answer with a story about selflessness or giving to others, they are likely to be considered a good fit. Such stories being passed around the organization have become part of the lore of Southwest.

ASB Bank (NZ) believes branded customer service has to be more than skin-deep. The bank has grown from a modest-sized regional savings bank to a front-runner, both in terms of market share and performance. For a number of years, it has consistently rated highest in customer satisfaction among full-service New Zealand banks.[7]

ASB expands its customer brand promise, "One Step Ahead," to its internal culture with the slogan "One Step Ahead—Through Our People." ASB places a strong emphasis upon repeatedly supporting and recognizing staff and committing to the skills and personal development of both its leadership and general staff.

"One Step Ahead" is a strong promise in the banking industry, but it is fair to say that ASB lives it consistently. ASB participated in TMI's international complaint management research survey. The study spanned fourteen countries and involved over two hundred organizations. ASB not only topped New Zealand ratings, but it also achieved the best results in the world.

What was even more telling (and surely a little unnerving for its competitors) was the way ASB reacted to receiving these results.

Following a presentation at which the results were announced, the ASB general manager for personal banking told a group of senior managers, "Congratulations, everyone. That's great." Then he added, "Now what can we do to improve further? We have fifteen minutes before we are scheduled to finish this meeting, so let's brainstorm some ideas."

In many organizations, such an announcement would have occasioned high fives and self-congratulations. Most staff probably would have concluded this was an area not requiring much future effort. Instead, it spurred ASB to further action. A short time later, ASB initiated new complaint-handling training interventions. When the research was repeated the following year, the result was a 23 percent improvement and a position on top of the list worldwide again. And once more, a similar reaction was heard: "So how are we going to keep one step ahead? And a big step at that."

Are ASB management and staff intellectually superior to their competitors? Not in our view. Their distinction is that virtually everyone has a clear and consistent view about what they stand for and their individual role in delivering it. Staff members also share a sense of belief and emotional connection to the brand and each other. It shows on their faces when you meet them in person, and this brand belief is typically delivered in their customer interactions.

Using a discovery process to get the brand

Many organizations simply assume that they need only tell managers what the brand is and show them advertising and branded literature in order for them to understand the implicit promise of the brand. We have heard HR professionals maintain that they have carried out the brand message because they put the logo on every printed document. These people are no doubt related to the marketing professionals who assume they need go no further than telling consumers what the brand is by inundating them with advertising messages.

The process is obviously more complex than that. Yet more often than not, organizations offer little more than lip service to the total effect the brand has. In all likelihood, each manager has his or her personal interpretation of the brand.

To create a brand-driven culture, we recommend starting with a discovery process to assess brand perceptions and the culture that underpins them. Organizational values are key. When we ask managers, "What are the values of your company?" often, perhaps after a slight hesitation, they point to posters on the walls depicting their mission, vision, and values and dutifully recite the words that are boldly displayed. Sometimes when the values are not posted on the wall, no one in the room can remember what they are.

When asked, "What do you mean by those values?" or "Can you give me examples of behaviors consistent with those values?" the hesitation is inevitably much longer. When we repeat this exercise with a number of people, the answers normally vary significantly. And more often than not, the answers given by the managers vary considerably from those of the staff they supervise. When we present these results to managers, they are often surprised. They wonder how people in their organization can hold such divergent views on subjects, "that have been on our walls for years."

True values of companies are expressed by the natural and spontaneous behaviors displayed by staff. The marketing department may say its commitment is to "customers first," but what that means may not have been defined in a way that fosters consistent understanding. As a result, values posters are frequently little more than attractive wall hangings.

A simple exercise can demonstrate the root cause of this problem. In a group session of fifteen to twenty people, display a word and ask each person to write down three meanings of that particular word.

The word *summer,* for example, elicits ideas and emotions that are significantly different and varied across even a small group of seemingly similar people. Here's a summary of results we got from one group of ten people about the word *summer*. It is easy to see how each answer relates to *summer*. It is also easy to see if these were interpretations of a single brand value how individual behaviors could likely go in a variety of directions.

WHAT DOES THE WORD "SUMMER" MEAN TO YOU—GIVE THREE WORDS

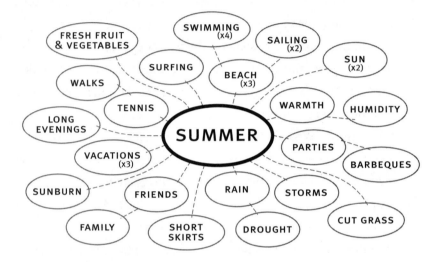

The reason words have different meanings to different people involves a range of factors, including past experiences, environment, preferences, ideals, and personal values. Each person's perception is specific to him or her. We might think that the word summer is quite straightforward and assume that everyone else is thinking the same thing when we say it. Is it any wonder that when an organization tells its employees it stands for customer service, trust, integrity, teamwork, and family, a clear and consistent understanding is lacking?

It is not shocking, therefore, that the behaviors demonstrated through customer service are often not consistent with the executives' or marketing department's interpretation of the brand. If an organization really wants its brand to be differentiated and delivered consistently, the brand cannot be left to general or individual inter-pretations. An organization must take responsibility to achieve clear understanding in the same way the marketing department assumes responsibility for stimulating specific awareness of the brand in con-sumers' minds.

This suggests two actions. First, the brand needs to be defined at a deeper level, explained and discussed within the specific context and offerings of the organization and based upon customer needs and aspi-rations. From there, the discussion can move to what the brand means to management and staff. Everyone needs to understand not just what the brand states in advertisements but also what these statements imply.

Managers must be directly engaged in this process, recognizing be-haviors that are on-brand and off-brand for a range of situations. Indi-vidual interpretations need to be aired, considered, and discussed. These things do not happen overnight. Even when the brand is well defined and communicated and staff are excited, change and brand awareness still grow slowly. That is precisely why well-recognized brands are so valuable.

What managers want and need to know about their brand

Based on our experience, managers—and staff for that matter—gen-erally have a similar set of questions about their brands (see table 6). Ideally, these questions should be answered on both a rational and an emotional basis.

Providing managers with rational answers may engage them at an intellectual level by telling them what they are required to do. If these questions are also answered with feelings taken into account, emo-tional connections can be created so that managers want to do what they need to do. It is at this level that engagement, and not just com-pliance, occurs.

Table 6. Questions about brand space

BRAND SPACE QUESTIONS	LOGICAL CONNECTION	EMOTIONAL CONNECTION	BRAND CONNECTION
WHAT ARE WE AIMING FOR?	*Goals*	*Meaningful purpose*	*Brand promise*
HOW WILL WE DO IT?	*Strategies*	*Shared values*	*Brand values*
WHAT'S MY ROLE?	*Tasks*	*Individual attitudes*	*On-brand behaviors*
ARE WE SERIOUS?	*Behaviors*	*Walking the talk*	*Brand integrity*
HOW ARE WE DOING?	*Measurement*	*Encouragement*	*Brand alignment*
WHAT'S THE RESULT?	*Compliance*	*Building commitment*	*Branded service*

Once you have defined the spirit of the brand and what it means in terms of behaviors, it needs to be inculcated into every possible form of organizational communication. Why? Because reiteration reinforces brand awareness and messages, as advertisers are quick to tell companies.

11

Selling in a Branded World: Linking Your Brand Proposition to Your Sales Messages

Before the concept of relationship marketing was introduced in 1975,[1] most sales were conceived of as short-term transactions, a "just get the orders" type of selling. Today, there is general agreement that relationship marketing (RM), where long-term relationships are formed, is the best sales model for strong brands.[2]

Marketing is, of course, closely related but not identical to sales. Marketing provides direction to sales, in great part through branding.[3] Sales, on the other hand, is the purpose of marketing.[4] Because of the hands-on nature of sales, sales departments must assume responsibility for ensuring sales teams follow marketing's direction and sell on-brand. Salespeople must understand that the way they sell is part of brand delivery and is part of a long-term strategic investment in the brand.

RM has as many definitions as there are people writing about the subject. The definition we are partial to is marketing expert Adrian Payne's, in which he explains that RM happens when marketing, customer service, and quality management intersect and has as its primary concern "the dual focus of getting and keeping customers."[5] Many "quality management" and "marketing" decisions occur outside the direct view of customers. Customer-staff interaction, on the other hand, is up-front, noticeable, and, as with most human-to-human interactions, complex to manage.

It used to be thought that relationship selling was necessary only when a sale was complex, customized, or conducted over a series of transactions. Today, we expect some type of relationship building even when the contact is minimal, such as when we purchase groceries. Most customers expect at least the relationship components of a smile and a greeting. As a result, many grocery store chains ask their checkers to use customers' names when handing them their receipts and to thank customers for their business.

How relationship marketing affects branding

A relationship approach to sales affects brand delivery in two ways: it implies service representatives have knowledge about customers, and it allows time for brand reinforcement.

Relationship marketing implies knowledge about the customer

Many organizations today possess intimate consumer knowledge stored online. Some customers know this and are worried, in fact, about how much is known about them. Domino's Pizza was an early adopter of a CRM phone system that actually tells the order taker who is calling. This enables Domino's to address the customer by name before the customer has said anything. Tim Monteith, vice president of information services, understands this might seem "invasive" to the customer.[6] When your brand promise is to be the world's best pizza delivery company, you have to be careful with information. As a result, Domino's employees are told to ask who is calling, even though they already know.

When customer information is used with respect and not abused, sales can be delivered with great personal impact, configured for each person and saving everyone a lot of time. Many Web sites create a feeling of relationship by greeting you with your name when you sign in and, in the case of Amazon.com, by recommending other books based on your selections. Are these real relationships? Most of us would say no, but they utilize information that makes them appear relationship based.

Long-lasting relationships are based on honesty and consistency. Both values are challenging for organizations to deliver because many customers today have their needs met through multiple service representatives. If representatives deliver inconsistent messages, this inconsistency will be interpreted as dishonesty or incompetence. Yet CRM technology promises, or at least implies, that every organizational representative who interacts with customers can have enough knowledge to create at least a minimal feeling of relationship. Our experience, however, is that when a service representative is busy reading a computer screen filled with information about you, unless that is done very carefully, it is difficult to experience a feeling of mutuality, let alone one that is on an equal basis. Customers, after all, do not have a parallel screen providing intimate information about the salesperson.

Selling creates time for reinforcing the brand

The sales experience generally takes time, during which a brand can be communicated and reinforced. This is true whether a sale is handled person-to-person or online. The sales experience, in fact, may be the longest opportunity the organization has to interact directly with a customer. When surveyed, customers say they expect the sales process to be part of the total experience of buying the brand.[7]

Many organizations are structured, however, so that sales are isolated from the total experience of the brand. But researchers know that if a customer has a negative experience while purchasing, it tends to linger while he or she is consuming the product or service. This can include an unpleasant experience buying admission to a theme park, placing an order with a snarling waiter, being checked into a hotel by a disinterested agent, getting your seating assignment at an airport, or handling insurance information at a hospital or health clinic. In this regard, any negative generic customer experience will reflect poorly on the total experience of a brand, even if the bad service is not specifically off-brand.

Customers report that most of their positive feelings for brands, in fact, come during the service process—not from the sales process.[8] If this is the case, a major opportunity to develop the brand is being missed. Yet business commentator Peter Jordan points out that salespeople frequently blame customer dissatisfaction on everyone but themselves. He writes, "If a business' primary overall objective is to retain its good customers, then its reward structure needs to be pegged to that objective, rather than heaping glory and reward on the rainmakers who bring in new accounts as in a front-end commission arrangement."[9] In this respect, the brand experience, the magic, must be integrated into the selling process. Clearly, hard sales techniques are outside the boundary of what customers want.

Your sales structures and systems impact the brand your customers are delivered

We know what customers want in the sales experience.[10] For purposes of this discussion, let's label these qualities as part of excellent generic selling:

- Trust
- Never sensing they have been cheated
- Feeling that the salesperson has a genuine concern for them
- Feeling very important
- Feeling at home

In addition, customers characterize high quality sales relationships as having the following:

- Positive attitudes
- Mutual flexibility
- Common vision and dreams
- Loyalty
- Mutual satisfaction

When customers do not receive what they expect in the sales process, as much of an opportunity is lost to strengthen the brand as when they do not receive what they were promised in the product and service delivery process.

In its attempts to imbue the sales experience with a specific brand essence, an organization must first determine if its internal systems and policies interfere with staff's ability to sell common brand qualities such as trust and personal concern. It's very easy for this interference to happen, as the following example demonstrates.

An acquaintance, Julia, sold for Nieman Marcus during a busy Christmas season. During orientation and training, she was instructed to stay with customers with whom she had created rapport and accompany them to other departments to help with additional sales. This is definitely a good idea, especially for a high-end retailer whose customers have been promised more personalized attention. It also utilizes relationship selling.

When Julia created such a relationship with her first customer, she asked if the woman needed help with anything else. The shopper said she wanted to buy something for her husband. Julia, according to her instructions, walked with the customer to the men's department and helped her with those purchases, which by that time were considerable.

Upon returning to her own department, Julia's supervisor asked her where she had gone. After explaining, Julia was curtly told, "I don't care what they told you in orientation. I don't make any commissions on what you sell in other departments. Don't leave this department ever again."

Consistency and on-brand selling

Obviously, when customers deal with a single salesperson, they can expect some degree of consistency. For this reason, many high-volume customers in business-to-business relationships demand one point of contact. They do this to ensure consistent answers; otherwise, customers may receive as many different answers as people with whom they speak. Low-volume, ordinary consumers cannot normally make this demand.

Consistency is important to customers as they seek a comfort level that is difficult to create when they are passed from one person to another. To the degree that an organization can create consistent customer relationships instead of customer transactions, it is a good strategy—especially if the brand promotes personalization.

on-brand

Janelle shops at a store selling one brand of high-quality German clothing and normally deals with the same salesperson each time. On the day after Christmas, when the store was filled with customers, another sales clerk walked up to her as soon as she entered the store, shook her hand, and said, "Hi, Janelle. Julie is not here today, so I'll help you today." And she did! When Janelle checked out her purchases, she was told, "I'll be sure to tell Julie you were in."

For many companies, this type of customer knowledge simply is not possible. For example, when you go to McDonald's, you rarely will place your order for a hamburger and a Coke with the same person you ordered from on your last trip to the Golden Arches. Under these circumstances, the sales process needs to be dissected and analyzed so that a consistent feeling can be created for customers—even if the customer is rarely known by name—whether this means always flashing a smile, offering a distinct greeting, or employing a process that feels familiar. Otherwise, customers are constantly walking into a "new" establishment, and they will not feel at home. Starbucks creates a consistent feeling very well in the way its staff call out each order to their coffee baristas. The order is precise: size, quality, style, and add-ons. Wherever you place an order at any Starbucks outlet, you will hear your request stated in the exact same order.

Delivering a consistent feeling creates a platform where previous positive emotions can be re-experienced. For example, if we want our customers to feel important and the most our staff will likely deal with the same person is once, then we must educate staff about how to be customer-centered, rather than self-centered or organization-centered. To do this requires education that goes way beyond taking an order, processing a request, knowing the price of merchandise, and understanding technical specifications of products. It requires a real emotional sophistication on the part of salespeople.

The genuine challenge for organizations is to educate hourly staff, many being paid at minimum wage, about the complexity of delivering human reactions that reinforce a brand. Dr. Maureen O'Hara, president of Saybrook Institute, throws the gauntlet down for modern organizations.

All this puts pressure on people to be a lot more psychologically flexible than ever before. People need what I call group empathy encompassing a whole set of higher-order mental skills; openness to learning, a capacity for self-criticism, low defensiveness, and the ability to process multiple realities and values.[11]

In addition, salespeople have to be effective communicators of the brand's attitudes, values, positioning, and promise. When you consider that most managers, and many executives, cannot tell you what their brand's attitudes, values, positioning, and promise are, we have a huge task ahead of us to get all levels of salespeople consistently communicating these messages.

Exercises follow in chapter 12 that will help your staff think through your sales process in relationship to your brand.

12

The Toolbox of On-Brand Exercises

When adapted to your particular brand and organizational culture, the exercises in this toolbox can start the process of helping your staff understand branding in general, your brand in particular, and their role in delivering it.

When reviewing this sampling, we recommend that you do not read the exercises one after another. They will blend into each other, lose meaningful context, and put your brain in process overload. We suggest you first determine what you want and need to accomplish. Then go to the toolbox, find headings that interest you, and choose what you need. Read those exercises carefully, and adapt them to your unique brand DNA.

You will need dozens of these types of exercises in order to maintain high levels of staff engagement with your brand. You don't want to repeat the same exercises over and over again. We collect exercises on our Web site, http://www.brandedservice.com. Our invitation to organizations and readers of this book is to share approaches they have devised so we can post them on our Web site. This way, every organization will have a brimming toolbox of exercises that can be adapted to its brand needs.

Brand awareness exercises for staff are divided into four categories:

- Brand knowledge: What are brands all about?
- Brand specificity: What is unique about our brand?
- Brand assessment: Are we on-brand or off-brand?
- Brand delivery: What does our brand look like in action?

On-brand exercises for managers are divided into three categories:

- Brand support for staff
- Brand reinforcement communication
- Brand alignment

Four exercises are also included to ensure your sales approach and messages are on-brand.

Brand awareness exercises for staff

The following exercises are designed to help your staff better understand the concept of branding in general and your own brand in specific. They will also help your staff develop a concrete sense of what it means to be on-brand or off-brand. Finally, these exercises will allow your staff to look at your brand from your customers' point of view.

Brand knowledge: what are brands all about?

Assist your staff with their general brand knowledge. Help them become knowledgeable of the role branding plays in business today. In the same way you ensure your staff know how to operate their computers, make sure they know at least as much about how brands operate. Remember, your brand may be your organization's most valuable asset. Protect it by investing in knowledge about the field of branding.

GENERAL BRAND KNOWLEDGE

A great deal can be learned about brands by simply studying the many strong brands that exist in today's marketplace.

- Ask your staff to list the characteristics of strong brands. Choose well-known brands such as Harley-Davidson or McDonald's, and ask them to figure out what makes them such strong brands.
- To increase awareness of taglines, find out how many well-known brand taglines they can recognize.
- Determine how many organizations they can identify merely by looking at the brand logos.
- Ask if they can state the brand promises of strong brands.
- Show examples of well-known service-related brands, such as entertainment parks, hotels, and fast-food restaurants. Ask about perceptions of these brands and then inquire how they arrived at their views. These questions will help your staff think about delivery of brand values connected to strong brand names.
- Build a brand resource center. Create a library of current books on branding. You can use the list at the end of this book as a start for

your collection. Post current news articles about brands on a bulletin board.

Wrap your staff in an environment that is imbued with information about branding. Just as you want your customers to have exposure to your brand as many times as possible, so, too, do you want to create multiple references to your brand or the topic of branding in general.

WHO OWNS OUR BRAND, AND WHAT DOES THIS MEAN?

Branding experts say that brands live in the minds of people. So at best, brands are co-owned, shared by the guardians of the brand (the organization) and the perceivers of the brand (consumers).

- Ask your staff for examples of products or services about which they feel a sense of ownership.
- Gather a number of printed ads of branded products. Ask who feels connected with any of them. Ask what this connection means to the strength of the brand.
- Then ask what type of reaction consumers have when they see your logo, product, or place of business.
- In a legal sense, the corporations own their brands; but in a figurative sense, consumers share ownership. Ask your staff to list all the implications if consumers, in fact, owned the brands.
- Discuss how your organization and its staff would behave differently if, in fact, the consuming public were literal owners of your brand. Would any of these changes be beneficial to your organization?

ON- AND OFF-BRAND SERVICE EXPERIENCES

The purpose of this exercise is to teach your staff the difference between generic service and branded customer service. This is a subtlety that your staff must learn to distinguish if they are going to be able to enhance your brand proposition with their own service and customer interactions.

Most customer service programs ask for examples of good and bad service. That's an important question, and people learn while discussing such examples. This exercise uses the same question but about branded service. When you first ask questions about on- and off-brand service experiences, people may not be able to think of a single example. They will no doubt think of dozens of examples of poor generic service but not necessarily off-brand service.

Let this discussion be an ongoing one to which you keep returning. Publish examples in your company newsletters. Post them on your intranet.

VISIT STRONGLY BRANDED COMPANIES

There are many examples of strongly branded organizations to visit. Check the Web site of any company you are going to visit so you have a strong sense of what it is trying to do. Your field trip will be more instructive.

One strongly branded company is the Great Harvest Bread Company, and you can visit one of its many shops. Here's the Great Harvest Bread Company's mission statement: "Be loose and have fun. Bake phenomenal bread. Run fast to help customers. Create strong & exciting bakeries. And give generously to others."

If you are not near one of Great Harvest Bread's 140 locations across the United States, find another strong brand and take your staff on a field trip. Ask them to observe

- how and which staff behavior contributes to the brand experience
- the total experience and whether it is on-brand or not
- any off-brand experiences

At Great Harvest Bread, observe if Pete Wakeman, one of its founders, has done what he writes about the company's mission: "Recruit the nicest, most generous, most honest and authentic people we can find—who love learning for the plain fun of it, who see business as an excuse to play, and love all of life for the sheer thrill of a bumpy ride—and bring them together in a caring community which supports these entrepreneurial types to TRULY run their own thing, make their own mistakes, have their own successes, and be 100 percent themselves."[1]

Brand specificity: what is unique about our brand?

Once your staff have a solid grasp of what a brand is, you can then use this base of knowledge to explore your own brand. The following exercises are concerned with your brand in specific.

WHO IS OUR BRAND?

Every time we see a group wrestle with the following brand exercise, we again are convinced of its value. This exercise enables people to put a human face on their brand.

- Ask your staff to identify your brand as a man or woman. Assign an age and give it a name. How educated is your brand?
- Have your staff think of your brand as a fully developed person who can be described in great detail. Harley-Davidson, for example, is probably not an elderly person or a young child. And even though many middle-aged men and women buy Harleys, the brand aspires to youth and freedom. When middle-aged people buy one of these powerful, rumbling motorcycles, they are buying a piece of youth and freedom.
- Have magazines available so people can create a collage that represents your brand.
- If your brand is going through a transformation, you can phrase the question, Who is our brand? in two ways: What is the brand right now as it appears to the public? And what do we want users of our brand to experience?

- In doing this exercise, it is likely your staff will begin to describe your actual organization, rather than your brand. Keep them focused on your brand or brands. If you need representation from the marketing department to help keep you brand focused, invite one of your brand experts to participate.

OUR BRAND IN THE FUTURE

This is an exercise to have your staff describe your brand in the future. Invite them to tell the story of your brand as it occurs over the next ten years.

Engaging in this type of projection encourages staff to see that they own your brand and its future as much as anyone or anything else does. To stimulate their thinking, ask your staff specific questions that relate to your brand, including future-based questions, such as the following:

- How many people recognize our brand logo? How did this happen?
- Our brand has gained the number one ranking in its market niche. What did we do to achieve this?
- We just won a major award for our brand. What was the award for and how did we win it?
- Three major newspaper features have appeared about the brand because of something that happened. All the stories were positive. What were they about?
- While our brand core has remained the same over the years, our brand has developed. What are some of these developments?
- What has been your role in our brand's future?

BRAND UNIQUENESS

If your brand stands for friendliness, you can be sure that a number of brands would also claim that. And many of them possibly are your direct competitors. What is it about your style of friendliness that is different from everyone else's? Is it the way you express it verbally? Is it the degree to which you apply friendliness as a concept? Is it overstated or subtle? If your friendliness is not different from everyone else's, then it is not a unique position.

The point of this process is to help your staff understand how your brand is differentiated not just by your logo and marketing material but by all the behaviors displayed to your customers.

- Divide your staff into groups and ask them to list all the features that are unique about your brand. If your company represents several brands, choose one at a time.
- Ask that all the answers be compiled on sticky notes (one unique characteristic per sticky note) and then organize them into categories.
- Have your staff challenge the unique identifiers of your brand, pointing out where other brands offer or do the same thing. The point of the exercise is to help your staff clearly understand the unique offerings of your brand.

OUR BRAND EMOTIONS

Because people have differing definitions of words, it can be helpful to have your staff develop a deeper appreciation for the emotional value your brand adds. One clever way to do this is to ask your staff to write down as many words that relate to or are synonymous with your brand values.

For example, let's say you want to provide a "refreshing" experience. When related words are presented, a much broader scope for *refreshing* can be imagined. In J. I. Rodale's *The Synonym Finder,*[2] you'll find words related to *refreshing,* including *renewing, reviving, stimulating, thirst-quenching, cooling, like a breath of fresh air, cheering, encouraging,* and *enheartening.*

- Choose a specific task accomplished for a customer that is relevant to your brand. For example, if you are a resort, checking in someone to the resort would be an appropriate task to select.

- Ask your staff to design a "refreshing" check-in process. Using the word *refreshing* might lead a group of people to think of a few specific actions that could be taken. But adding phrases such as *stimulating, cooling, thirst-quenching,* and *like a breath of fresh air* could unleash the creative power of your staff to think of dozens more related experiences that would enable customers to experience your brand.

Brand assessment: are we on-brand or off-brand?

One of the important concepts covered in this book is the idea of "on-brand" and "off-brand." The following exercises are designed to help your staff pay attention to how their service behavior either supports your brand promise or fails to deliver it.

CUSTOMER TOUCH POINTS: ARE WE ON-BRAND OR OFF-BRAND?

Make a list of interactive customer touch points, all the Moments of Truth your customers have with your organization. Then ask, "Is the way we do this on-brand or off-brand?" If you are already largely on-brand, then ask, "How can we do this so it is *even more* on-brand?"

For example, on page 46 we described an experience a customer had on a luxury cruise line. At the end of the trip, customers were asked to evaluate the trip. The evaluation asked for the guests to write in their own names, cabin number, and the date. Prior to the evaluation, customer touch points had been highly personalized.

To be more consistent with the brand, a form that already had the passenger's name written (by hand!) would have shown personalization. (And to anticipate those who would not fill out a feedback form with their name on it, the form could have been perforated so their name could be easily removed.) For greater impact, the form could have been presented on lovely paper to show that the cruise line valued his or her input. And a stamp could have been placed on the envelope in case the passenger preferred to send it from shore.

Ask your staff what they would do to make their Moments of Truth on-brand. It is possible that in the cruise ship example, the staff may have decided that the evaluation feedback form was not where they wanted to put efforts to make the brand come alive. After all, a regular evaluation form is not bad service. Should we do this? is an important question when making decisions to implement brand practices. As there are limitless numbers of actions employees can take to be on-brand, they need to prioritize according to impact and time demands.

CUSTOMER SURVEYS

Most organizations conduct customer surveys. Very frequently these surveys do not measure whether your brand is being delivered. The survey described below enables your staff to receive direct information from your customers as to how you are delivering your brand and to determine what your brand means to your customers.

- Ask your staff to call three to five of your customers this week. If this is difficult, these surveys can also be conducted whenever staff talk with customers. A telephone call isn't the only way to get the information you want.
- Ask customers what they think your brand represents.
- Learn which emotions they associate with your brand.
- Ask what your customers like about your brand.
- Find out if your customers ever received service they thought was in direct opposition to your brand promise.

As a matter of course, it would be a good idea for staff to ask these questions of customers whenever appropriate. This habit continually engages both staff and customers about brand issues.

If you have some token that is related to your brand, you could offer it as a thank-you to your customers for their information.

EMPOWERMENT AND OUR BRAND

We are acquainted with a company that sells multimillion-dollar software and hardware interventions. Yet any package requiring over $25 in delivery charges must be approved by the salesperson's direct manager before being sent. Late on Friday afternoons, many managers have already left the office or are out of town. If a customer calls with an immediate need that requires shipping costs over $25, an empowerment issue is created. At this particular company, staff follow the requirement for getting approval rather than taking care of customer needs. They place the paperwork on the appropriate manager's desk for his or her return and approval—on Monday morning or later.

This action means the company's brand promise is regularly compromised when a customer has an emergency on a Friday afternoon and the remedy requires a delivery charge that exceeds $25. The staff in this company are no longer upset about the practice. They have learned to let a manager talk to the irate customer on Monday. The staff, unfortunately, have lost their personal identification with the brand promise of taking care of needs immediately. When asked about this situation, the managers say that they have no choice. They are being pressured by senior management to bring costs under control, and this is one way to fix the problem.

- Ask your staff what services they provide that require a manager's approval or intervention. Managers typically miss the impact of most approval requirements because they more likely focus on how the approval process keeps matters under control, rather than how it negatively impacts brand delivery.

- Once you have identified the empowerment limitations placed on your staff, analyze each situation through the lens of how this impacts brand delivery. When you find a conflict (and your staff will tell you if you give them an opportunity to speak out), aim for one goal: minimize the number of people customers must speak with to get their needs met.

LIVING OUR BRAND INSIDE OUR ORGANIZATION

This exercise will enable your staff to consider how your brand values are followed within your organization. Not only will the exercise open up a discussion about the relationship between organizational culture and brand delivery, but it is also possible that managers will receive valuable information from their staff about what is required to support the brand internally.

- Ask your staff to describe all the ways in which your brand is currently lived *inside* your organization. Use one sticky note per description so you can easily group their responses.

- Then ask them to write what they like best about working for your organization. Again, write one response per sticky note. Expect some answers to be that the best thing about work is making money. Obviously, earning money is important. In fact, you might wish to anticipate this response by writing it down as a first example.

- Finally, ask your staff to list the three actions they think your organization needs to take in order to live the brand internally. Do this exercise in groups, and you will be rewarded with a serious discussion of the issue.

The key to these questions is to help staff see that their jobs are about much more than merely completing tasks or simply making money. From the customers' viewpoint, service jobs ultimately are brand related. If staff develop an on-brand mind-set, service-related tasks will be performed to a higher standard.

Brand delivery: what does our brand look like in action?

THE EXPERIENCE NEEDS OF OUR CUSTOMERS

This is a multistep exercise to get to the heart of what your customers would like to experience with your brand.

- First, list experiences your customers want (their needs) in relationship to something you do for your customers.
- Second, describe these needs using your customers' voices.
- Third, list specific ways your organization or team can meet these needs as they relate to your brand values.

Table 7 shows a sample of how a company that produces training seminars and related materials might answer the above questions.

BRAND SKILLS AND RESOURCES

Most organizations assess internal training needs from time to time. After your staff understand your brand and know what they need to do to deliver it, ask them what specific skills and resources they need to better deliver the brand.

Here are a few possibilities that may never show up in a regular needs assessment list.

- Acting classes
- Language or elocution training
- Penmanship instruction
- Personal image and professional presence training
- Memory classes for name retention

- Humor classes
- Emotional competency skills
- Cross-cultural understanding
- Seminar on reading body language
- Foreign language skills
- Brand-related selling skills
- Specific product experience

Table 7. A sample brand in action

CUSTOMER SERVICE EXPERIENCES:
PROGRAMS AND PRINTED MATERIALS

THE NEED	NEEDS DESCRIPTION IN OUR CUSTOMERS' VOICES	POSSIBLE WAYS TO MEET THE NEED AS IT RELATES TO OUR BRAND
Reliability of our printed materials	*We want materials to be of the highest quality—as promised. This means no errors and timely delivery.*	*Always have two people check our completed work. Let customers know we take the extra time to double-check our printed materials. If we find any significant errors, reprint the material at no extra cost to the client.*
Innovative, most recent ideas in our programs and printed materials	*If we wanted rehashed ideas or copies of materials from the Internet, we'd do it ourselves. We are hiring you to buy your creativity, uniqueness, and inspiration.*	*We spend time in brainstorming ideas; we do not copy our competitors' work; we always tweak our materials so even if a similar process or idea is used, it is customized to precisely fit each client. We let our customers know when we have developed something specifically for them.*

Another way to approach this is to identify the people on staff who best deliver your brand. Study them and note the unusual talents or skills they possess. Then replicate these abilities in the rest of your staff through training. Encourage your talented brand deliverers to become mentors to new staff.

IDEAL BRAND BEHAVIOR, ACTUAL BRAND BEHAVIOR

Apply a quality technique to your brand delivery.

- First, define customer interactive touch points.
- Then identify specific on-brand behaviors for each touch point.
- Next, describe what ideal brand behavior (IBB) would look like.
- Then describe your actual brand behavior (ABB). (You may need to send in undercover shoppers to measure your actual delivery levels.)
- The difference between the IBB and the ABB is the gap you want to close. Involve staff to help you describe precisely what needs to be done to reach the IBB level.

SEQUENCING OF IDEAS

Psychologists know that the order in which they ask their questions influences the answers that people give.[3] This happens at an unconscious level through a phenomenon called *priming,* in which our brains are made ready for an idea by the order in which items are presented.

You can influence answer choice by presenting a nonverbal cue and then asking someone a question. Bring up a pizza reference in conversation with someone, for example, and then ask what kind of food that person would like for dinner. There's a good chance that he or she will choose pizza because you stimulated the idea of pizza in the person's brain.

Choose a process that you follow with your customers and experiment with the order in which you go through the process. Seek to understand if the order of presentation makes a difference in customer behavior or reactions. For example, most toll-free customer service help desks start with identification questions, which are not the most brand-reinforcing questions.

The unspoken message conveyed by the order in which you ask for information may say that you are more interested in your procedures than you are in listening to customers so you can help them. Our own experience tells us that asking identification questions first primes many customers to heightened levels of irritation.

USING LANGUAGE TO ENHANCE OUR BRAND EXPERIENCE

Fabulous Freddy's gas stations in Las Vegas encourage staff to say "fabulous" when they can naturally interject the word in conversations with customers. Ask them how they are, and they will tell you, "Fabulous." It's obvious what they are doing, and it's also fun. Indeed, "fabulous" seems to affect their whole demeanor. They rush to offer to pump gas at no extra charge.

Reinforcement of Fabulous Freddy's brand through language makes it easy for customers to remember them, especially since every time you go for a car wash you will hear, "Have a *fabulous* day."

Choose one of the words contained in your brand promise and ask your staff to experiment with ways to naturally use that word in your customer communications. For example, if your brand contains the emotion word *exciting,* how can that word be "naturally" integrated into your conversations with customers?[4] The key is to make the use of your brand words not sound forced but rather delivered in such a way to reinforce the brand promise. Here are some examples using the word *exciting/excited:*

- Leaving a message on a voice mail system: "Mr. Roberts, I have some *exciting* news. I believe I have a solution to the question you phoned about. Thank you and please call me at ******."

- Helping a customer make a clothing purchase: "I think you'll be excited about how easy this fabric is to care for. You can literally throw it in the laundry and then wear it right away."

- Setting up an appointment: "Well, this is *exciting.* I can work you in this afternoon. Can you make it over here by then?"

BEHAVIORALLY DEMONSTRATING BRAND VALUES TO CUSTOMERS

Many organizations take care of customers' needs at counters staffed with multiple service providers. Under such circumstances, it is not uncommon to see an employee working on a computer behind a Closed sign—even if customers are waiting in a long line.

While the customers have no way of determining what that person is doing at the computer, it looks as if the organization has higher priorities than reducing the waiting time that customers are forced to spend to get help.

- Choose one of your brand values that has strong behavioral implications, such as responsiveness, respect, or dignity.

- Ask your staff to brainstorm all the ways you can behaviorally show your customers you are responsive to them, respect them, or treat them with dignity.
- Make a parallel list of all the behaviors customers will likely interpret as nonresponsive, disrespectful, or undignified treatment.

BRAND CUES

Many large institutions have little regard for their patrons' time, as witnessed by poor or inadequate signs. For example, we have yet to hear anyone talk about the Grand Ole Opry Hotel in Nashville, Tennessee, without mentioning how difficult it is to find one's way around that sprawling property.

Cues speak volumes about your brand delivery—even if customers are not consciously aware of them. Professor Gerald Zaltman provides an example of this type:

> Something as simple as a wall clock included in a magazine-ad photo can exert a powerful impact on what consumers retain about the ad. For example, a picture of someone being helped at a service counter in a setting where a wall clock is displayed is more than twice as likely to evoke the notion of speedy service than the same image without the wall clock.[5]

Here are three ideas to consider when looking at your brand cues.

- Identify brand cues that relate to your brand values. Divide them into categories and tackle them group by group.
- Advertisers use inserts in Sunday newspapers to cue customers to come to their stores. What cues can you use to let customers know

you are serious about your brand values once they arrive at your location? For example, what do your staff titles (and name badges) tell customers about your brand or how you treat your staff?

- Pay attention to your cues that send negative messages. For example, if you occupy a large location, do your direction signs let your customers—and staff—know you are concerned about their time? Or does the absence of signs or poorly placed signs send the negative message that you don't really care whether they get lost?

COMPLAINT HANDLING AND OUR BRAND

Service recovery, or complaint handling, is a huge issue for brands. As a result of looking thoroughly at this topic for over ten years, we know that one of the easiest times to be off-brand is when customers voice complaints. There are so many ways to be off-brand in these situations.

- Ask your staff how they can handle complaints while remaining on-brand. To keep your discussion brand focused, talk about effective complaint handling that stays on-brand, rather than just effective complaint handling.

- Ask your staff to pretend they are a customer with a fairly common problem. Have them imagine calling your organization and asking for help with a complaint. Then ask, "What would customers expect from you so you are consistent with your brand even though the customer found something to complain about?"

- Can your staff figure out ways to link your brand promise to your style of complaint handling? For example, when alternatives are available that would help customers avoid recurring problems, would it enhance certain aspects of your brand promise to suggest them?

If lengthy lines plague your business, could your staff offer alternative times to visit your business when lines are not so long? This type of suggestion could be linked to a brand that offers size while emphasizing personal care.

- If your brand promise is about care, would it be appropriate for your staff to show empathy when customers face problems that no one can solve? For example, airlines frequently must deal with displaced passengers who cannot get home because of bad weather. While not the airlines' fault, a show of empathy can demonstrate caring.

- When customers complain about prices, staff need to know how to respond by selling brand value—not just value but value specifically linked to the brand. Do your staff know how to do this?

On-brand exercises for managers

These exercises are designed for managers to consider how your organizational culture impacts branded service delivery by your staff. They
consider staff support, communication about the brand, and brand
alignment with your mission and vision.

Brand support for staff

If your staff do not work in an environment that reflects your brand
promise, it will be difficult to gain their support for branded customer
service. How you reward and recognize your staff, recruit for new
staff, and conduct performance reviews all impact whether you can
feel assured that staff will deliver your brand—even when you are not
there to supervise service behavior.

REWARDS AND RECOGNITION

Most managers understand the importance of rewarding and recognizing the actions they want taken. In a branded service environment,
rewarding and recognizing specific brand-coherent behaviors is extremely important. If "generic" service behaviors are recognized, then
staff will tend to deliver these. But when specific branded service
behaviors are recognized, such as those described below, there is a
much greater likelihood that staff will pay attention to delivering your
brand while offering service to customers.

- How does your management team recognize and then reward on-
  brand behaviors? In order to be more conscious about this, first
  identify what on-brand staff behaviors look like.

- Then be on the lookout for these behaviors so they can be specifically recognized.
- Sit down at the end of each week and recall when you saw staff, colleagues, and upper management be brand consistent. Note at least five examples of on-brand behavior. Throughout the next week, say something about what you saw. For example, to an employee of a salon named The Glass Ceiling: "Good work. I noticed the way you complimented Ms. Jordan after she had her makeup and hair done. You told her she looked 'Serene, confident, and very professional.' I'll bet that meant something significant to her as she was just promoted to her first executive position. Your statement really highlighted the salon's brand of 'Taking you higher as you move up.' Good work!"
- Consider whether it would be a good idea for your organization to link specific rewards to demonstrations of on-brand behavior. For example, if you promise "unlimited possibilities," could your rewards be linked to when that happens?

STAFF RECRUITMENT

If you could hire people who possess specific qualities to represent your brand, for what qualities would you look? Make a list of these, and then explore how you can test for these qualities.

If "helpfulness" is part of your brand promise, for example, could you set up a test so that applicants walk past someone who is struggling to lift a heavy object? See how many applicants stop to help the person.

If you can hire people who have a natural resonance with your brand, half the battle is won in terms of encouraging them to consistently deliver on-brand interactions.

ON-BRAND PERFORMANCE REVIEWS

Most managers struggle with performance reviews. When asked to write them in an on-brand manner, they *really* struggle. The review process needs to be broken down and carefully explained, and examples need to be provided for managers to see that performance reviews can be as much a part of supporting the brand promise as anything else.

To begin with, what are you measuring in your performance reviews? Are you measuring the same behaviors that you promise your customers? That is a good beginning point.

Get a group of managers together and ask them to brainstorm all the possible ways to conduct on-brand performance reviews. Questions to consider include the

- frequency of reviews
- style (360 degrees, in person, written)
- location (Where are the reviews conducted? You send a negative message about staff development if you conduct your performance reviews in the hallways whenever you can catch people.)
- rewards

HUMAN RESOURCE POLICIES

Take a look at all your personnel policies to see whether they interfere with on-brand behaviors.

- Are your HR policies aligned with your brand?
- Do you tie the hands of your staff with internal rules that make it difficult for them to deliver on-brand service?
- Are your policies brand friendly?
- Does your brand stress possibilities you create for your customers, while you, at the same time, behave restrictively toward staff? We know one internationally branded shop that emphasizes "unique possibilities" for a shopping experience, while the clerks' handbags are searched for stolen articles as they leave at the end of the day.
- If part of your brand promise necessitates empowered staff for delivery of that promise to your customers, how do your HR policies support the required empowerment? For example, if staff make mistakes in their empowered decisions, how are they treated? Can you and do you fire staff for these types of mistakes? Or are mechanisms in place to allow staff to learn from these mistakes?

ADVERTISING AND TRAINING RATIO

An internal branding process can be carried out for the same cost as a few major ad placements or campaigns. Consider that one off-brand experience can be repeated dozens of times, perhaps spreading far wider through word of mouth than the single showing of a television ad. And people believe their own experiences more than an ad. After all, they reason, the company has a vested interest in advertising itself in the best light. What really counts is what they experience and what their friends and family say.

Multiple surveys suggest that organizations spend a great deal more money on advertising and marketing than they do on staff training, especially brand values training.

- Ask your department heads and human resource personnel how much money they spend on training (separate out technical skills training from service or brand training) in one year.

- Compare this figure with your marketing and advertising budget. No doubt the correct ratio needs to be a floating ratio, but if you look at the two figures and say, "Something is not right here," it probably isn't!

Reinforcement communication

Any solid management intervention requires reinforcement. The following four ideas can help you to focus your communication so it reinforces your brand every time you communicate with your staff.

DESIGNING ON-BRAND INTERACTIONS WITHIN THE ORGANIZATION

Choose one of the emotions or elements of your brand, and ask questions about a range of interactions you have with your staff and colleagues. If the brand value is "excitement," for example, sample questions might include the following:

- How can we lead exciting staff meetings?
- Are our internal communications exciting? How can we make them more exciting?
- How can we convey excitement in the first few minutes when we enter the office or greet our customers?
- Is there some way we can make payday even more exciting?
- Does our office design look exciting? How about the paint on the walls? Is it exciting?

ADVERTISEMENTS AS PART OF YOUR INTERNAL COMMUNICATION

Get your management team involved to determine how effectively your ads communicate with your staff.

- Do you first sell your ads internally before releasing them publicly? A good reason for testing them internally is that your ads may strike a raw nerve that can actually demotivate your staff. We know of one company that emphasized its total commitment to its customers.

The idea behind the ads was this company's employees did nothing but work twenty-four hours a day to (breathe, eat, sleep, drink) solve customer problems. The backlash was palpable. One wife of a midlevel manager told her husband, "Well, they finally got it right. That's exactly what you do." Some customers even commented they preferred a supplier that encouraged staff to have more balanced lives. A preview of the ad concept to staff could have prevented hearing about this slant on the ads only after they were already produced and rolled out.

- Do you show your ads to your staff? If repetition is one of the keys to brand reinforcement, then showing or displaying your ads to staff on every appropriate occasion is simply taking advantage of awareness, reinforcement, and culture building. There is no excuse for customers to be better acquainted with your organization's advertisements (whether on television or as a flyer inserted into the Sunday newspapers) than your staff.

Unfortunately, most consumers have had the experience of needing to educate staff about special offers that have been widely advertised. There is something very off-brand when a clerk has to reach for a flyer to see what specials are being offered this week. Several messages are sent with this type of behavior: (1) we do not know the value of items we sell; (2) if customers fail to be diligent, they will be charged regular and not sale prices; (3) things change so frequently around here, we are not able to keep up with them.

INTERNAL INFORMAL BRAND-STRATEGY SURVEY

Conduct an informal survey among the people who report to you. Ask them about their strategy to ensure your brand values are met during all customer interactions.

If they give you examples of specific steps that they take to be on-brand, steer them back to your question about strategy. Strategy is long-term and aspirational and generally looks at the situation from thirty-five thousand feet.

While you are in conversation with your immediate subordinates, ask them how one of your brand values (take a rather common one, such as trust) is differentiated from this same value as expressed by one of your major competitors. If they tell you it is more or less the same, it is time to work on how your brand is differentiated, lived, and then delivered!

BRAND BOOKS

When technology services company Comdisco rebranded itself, it printed a Brand Book for thirty-five thousand employees. Comdisco wanted to reflect the rapid changes in the field of technology both to employees and to customers. One Comdisco ad showed a small boy aggressively holding a sword, with the headline "I need constant attention. I am technology." Children are frequently used in Comdisco ads to emphasize constant change and experimentation.

Comdisco's Brand Book spells out how employees can embrace the company's brand position to deliver the promise of technology:

*"Become a brand champion with everyone—with customers and pros-
pects, your fellow employees, your friends and family. In short, live the
brand."* That is not mincing words![6]

If your organization has not published and distributed a Brand
Book, make it a priority. (More information about Brand Books can be
found in chapter 9.)

- Brand Books can contain much of the same information that your
  brand advertising messages sell, though it needs to have a staff slant
  to it.

- Make your Brand Book reflect your brand. If your brand is colorful
  and quirky, then use graphics that are fun and edgy. If your brand
  is more formal, design your Brand Book the same way.

Brand alignment

This book is, to a large degree, about brand alignment: aligning the brand with the mission, the vision, advertising, supplier relationships, and survey measurements. The following exercises will help your management team consider possible ways that your brand can be better aligned with everything you do as an organization.

MISSION, VISION, BUSINESS STRATEGY, AND BRAND ALIGNMENT

At least once a year (preferably at an off-site retreat so you can really focus on the topic), look carefully at your mission, vision, and business strategy. See how they line up with the changes that have taken place with your brand over the past year.

- Is your brand pulling you away from your mission and vision or vice versa?
- How does your business strategy support your brand strategy?
- Where is it off course?
- Ask your marketing department to provide you with data to help you see precisely what is happening with this important alignment.

ADVERTISING AND YOUR BRAND DELIVERY

Collect copies of your television, print, and radio advertising. Pretend you are an outsider being introduced to your company. What does your advertising tell you that you could expect from your organization if you were a customer?

- Make a checklist of your expectations.

- Invite a team of people to conduct this exercise so you have a variety of responses to consider.
- Ask several people to be mystery shoppers of your organization. For example, they could call your telephone numbers, visit your stores, send an e-mail question to your information desk, or order something online from your Web site.
- Check off the items in your expectations list to see how close your organization is to delivering the brand promises that are promoted in your advertising.

ARE YOUR SUPPLIER PARTNERS ON-BRAND?

Your suppliers have the potential to impact your brand as strongly as any of your staff. This exercise will enable you to assess whether your supplier partners are on-brand or off-brand.

- Make up a list of your suppliers. (If you need to talk with someone in your organization who knows these suppliers, do that.) You want to find out how close your suppliers are to your own brand values. If there is a big disconnect, there will no doubt be some contamination of the on-brand interactions you are attempting to create for your customers. This is particularly true if your customers need to deal with your suppliers in their total product or service experience. For example, some companies outsource their product service contracts. When your customers have a problem with the service provider, they do not distinguish between one of your suppliers and you.
- Insist that your suppliers deliver their services or products to you in the same way you deliver your services and products to your own

customers. You may need to set up a brand orientation for your suppliers when you sign contracts with them.

- While studying your suppliers, investigate how you treat them. It is difficult for suppliers to be consistently on-brand with you if you mistreat them. TMI has clients who expect immediate action from us. They tell us that is what they deliver to their customers. Yet we can make dozens of phone calls to them that go unanswered and write countless e-mails that are not responded to. When we finally do reach such a company's representatives, they assure us they are very sorry this has happened, but then they repeat the behavior. It makes us wonder what they do to their customers.

USING METRICS THAT MEASURE WHAT YOU WANT TO ACCOMPLISH

The old maxim "What gets measured is what earns attention" applies here. If you believe that being on-brand is critical to your organization, are you measuring specific customer reactions to your brand behaviors? In fact, very few companies do this. Rather, they ask customers if they are *satisfied*, a word that many psychologists doubt is an emotion at all. Satisfaction is probably an intellectual judgment. We also know how meaningless it is in driving loyalty.

Brand-engaged customers are loyal customers.

- Visit departments that are gathering data about your organization.
- Carry a checklist of brand promises, emotions, and values with you.
- Ask what is being measured, and then ask to see the data. Carefully consider it so everyone knows you take it seriously.

Ensuring your sales approach and messages are on-brand

Salespeople can easily adopt the attitude that their job is to "sell" and everyone else in the organization has the responsibility to ensure the brand is delivered. These four exercises can be used with a sales force to heighten their awareness about their role in delivering the brand promise while selling the brand.

CLUTTER REMOVAL

Examine everything your salespeople do for customers. Eliminate activities that are not necessary or not directly related to selling your brand promise or brand value to customers. This will, no doubt, require elimination of certain administrative tasks.

If you have an automated telephone system, do you make your customers identify themselves by their ID numbers and then ask for the same information again when they are connected to a live person? If so, eliminate that "clutter." How many times do you make customers sign your forms? Is that necessary for legal purposes? If not, eliminate that clutter.

Spend time with salespeople observing how their activities enhance your brand. Many times salespeople get confused as to what they are doing with customers. They don't frame their sales interactions to underscore the brand. Help them pare down their selling activities so your brand values create brand-reinforcing customer interactions. Keep them focused with clutter removal.

DEMAND CONSISTENCY

Identify which of your sales staff currently sell your brand values along with selling products or services. Set up step-by-step checklists of your already-successful sales staff so that your entire sales force can more easily emphasize all the essential points that relate to brand value.

We do not recommend scripting staff. We also appreciate that every salesperson has a slightly different style when he or she sells. However, some elements of your brand value should be influencing everyone's sales process.

Ask your salespeople to represent your brand's essential features— every time they sell! For example, if you deliver a product that is highly customized and this customization is one of your major brand propositions, sales messages about that customization should probably be presented within the first few minutes of any sales conversation.

SELL THE WAY YOUR CUSTOMERS LIKE TO BUY

Study your customers to find out how they like to buy your brand. What values are reinforced in the way they purchase your product so they are, in effect, purchasing your brand in the process of buying your products or services?

Most organizations know how they want their products to be sold without taking into consideration how the customer likes to buy. Telemarketers are renowned for this. For example, when we tell telemarketers that we are not interested in their products or services, they frequently still ask us to write down a toll-free number—in case we change our minds! All this does is increase irritation levels and reflect badly on the brand.

The purpose of branding is to reinforce the ideas that are meaningful to your customers even during the sales experience. Here are several questions to ask about customers to help you get started:

- Are there any parts of your brand that are not demonstrated in the sales process?
- Are your customers quick to make their decisions while buying from you? Or do they like a leisurely sell or some combination of both? How can you tell which customers want which selling style?
- What previous experience have customers had with you that you definitely do not want reinforced?
- What is of value (for example, education about your brand and products) to the customer in your sales process? How do these value points link to your brand promise?[7]

SELL YOUR BRAND

Make sure that your entire sales force knows how to sell your brand, without selling a service or product. In other words, if you were to sell the value of your brand idea, how would that be done?

Have one group of salespeople demonstrate selling just your brand. Have another group demonstrate selling your competitor's brand.

Learning how to focus on just your brand idea teaches salespeople to cut to the quick in terms of your brand values and proposition.

To do this, they will probably need to know your major brand stories. Some of them are legendary in companies; they are a treasure, and everyone who sells the company should know how to tell them in an exciting, engaging manner.

Final Thoughts

Customers have been teaching us for some time that generic service, even if it is excellent, no longer excites them. Generic service has become the vanilla flavor equivalent of connecting with customers. Generic service inspires judgments of satisfaction, a judgment that lacks the punch to create engaged and brand-loyal customers.

Branding your service experiences in all the myriad ways that are possible takes the discussion about customer service to its next logical step. Specifically, how can your organization use the concept of brand to align your promises to consumers, to live values you aspire to, and to deliver service experiences that customers need to receive if they are to remain your long-term customers?

When promises are aligned with service, you not only magnify your brand promise, but you also give your customers the service you promised them.

Throughout this book we have profiled a number of companies that have succeeded, by and large, in aligning customer service with their brand promises and values. However, regardless of how successful you become in building an on-brand organization, there will be times when you fall short of the standards you aspire to. It is a reality of the complex and fast-moving world we live in that mistakes are made, suppliers let us down, processes develop faults, or employees simply have a bad day. This is when the brand lens through which your service is viewed needs to be in its sharpest focus.

How you recover from these failures is integral to building trust with your customers. We have stated that without trust it is impossible to build strong, enduring emotional connections between customers and brands. Trust is based on the congruence between what your brand stands for and what you reliably do. It is also built upon openness and integrity.

Therefore, when you are off-brand, be honest with your customers. They will appreciate it. Honesty provides a great opportunity to not only restore customer faith but also to reinforce what your brand is— what you stand for and who you are.

The journey to an integrated brand, where the behavior of the organization matches its public promises, is complex. But no one has ever argued that a strong brand is an easy goal to achieve. At least we have a road map to get us moving in that direction.

Notes

Introduction: On-Brand or Off-Brand

1 We have been given permission to share this research on the condition that we do not name the bank involved.

2 As quoted in an interview on NPR, September 9, 2003.

3 James H. Gilmore and B. Joseph Pine II, "The Experience IS the Marketing," *Strategic Horizons LLP,* 2002.

4 See Craig Reynolds, "Boids: Background and Update," http://www .red3d.com/cwr/boids/ and Yuhai Tu and John Toner, "How Birds Fly To-gether: Long-Range Order in a Two-Dimensional Dynamical XY Model," *Physical Review Letters* 75 (December 4, 1995): 4326–4329.

5 Private interview, New Orleans, July 2003.

6 James Collins, *Good to Great* (New York: Harper Business, 2001), 14.

7 Bob Tyrell and Tim Westall, "The New Service Ethos, A Post-Brand Future—And How to Avoid It," *Market Leader: The Journal of the Marketing Society,* no. 2 (1998).

Chapter 1: The Branding Imperative

1 In a 2000 market survey, Brand Finance reported that "77 percent of ana-lysts and 77 percent of companies believe that branding will become [even] more important in the next five years." "The Case for Brand Value Report-ing," Research 2000, Brand Finance, http://www.brandfinance.com.

2 "The Brand Resilience Presentation," http://www.BrandGuardians.com.

3 OgilvyOne's research, as reported by Annick Deseure, "In Search of Under-standing," *Admap* (December 1999).

4 As reported by Bruce Horovitz, "Who Said That? Buyers Don't Recognize Some Slogans," *USA Today,* Money section, October 1, 2003.

5 Horovitz, "Who Said That?"

6 Martin Grant and Tim Opie, "Making More Than a Difference," *Admap* (April 2001).

7 The "gray zone" is David Haigh's term. Haigh offers three basic branding tests: the grayness test, the nonentity test, and the simpleton test. David Haigh, "Service Branding," Professional Marketing (2000), http://www .warc.com.

8 This comment was made after the Body Shop began to lose its consumers between the ages of twenty and thirty. See "Body Shop's Roddick Stands by Her Brand," *Sunday Post Online,* October 14, 2001.

9 Susan Fournier, "Consumers and Their Brands: Developing Relationship Theory in Consumer Research," *Journal of Consumer Research* 24 (March 1998): 365.

10 Visit http://www.starship.org.nz and take the interactive tour to get a sense of how different this hospital is.

11 S. and B. Richardson, Rotorua, *Sunday Star Times,* May 11, 2003.

12 Paraphrased from Strategem Limited's Web site, http://www.strategem .co.nz.

13 Philip Ross, "Branding," http://www.business-specialties.com/branding2 .htm.

14 Wendy Gordon and Sally Ford-Hutchinson, "Brains and Brands: Re-thinking the Consumer," *Admap* (January 2002).

15 Sam Hill, president of Helios Consulting, as cited in "The History of Brand-ing," http://www.studeografix.com.

16 For a complete discussion, see Douglas B. Holt, "Why Do Brands Cause Trouble? A Dialectical Theory of Consumer Culture and Branding," *Journal of Consumer Research* 29 (June 2002).

17 As quoted in "The Advertising Age," http://www.adage.com/century/ century.html.

18 J. Robinson, *The Economics of Imperfect Competition* (London: Macmillan, 1933).

19 Laura Barton, "Fascinated with Fake," *The Age* (August 26, 2003): 4.

20 Sylvia LaForet and John Saunders, "Managing Brand Portfolios: How the Leaders Do It," *Journal of Advertising Research* 34, no. 5 (September-October 1994): 64.

21 Morgan has codified the components of three major emotional factors (authority, identification, and social approval) that make a customer identify with one brand over another—even when they are basically the same. Morgan teases out this distinctive customer behavior as follows: authority (heritage: lengthy reputation; trust: reliability; innovation: seen as "leading edge"); identification (bonding: emotional comfort; level of care: understanding of needs; nostalgia: memories from the past); and social approval (prestige: upmarket, upscale, premium; acceptability: approval by peers; endorsement: used by respected people). Rory Morgan, "Towards the Development of New Tools for Measuring Brands," *Brand Strategy* (September 28, 1998).

22 Max Blackston, president, Research International, has carved out an area of expertise within the branding area specifically looking at how brands perceive the customer. See "The Levels of Brand Power," *Admap* (March 1993).

23 See Alan Mitchell, Right Side Up (New York: Harper Collins Business, 2000), and John Grant, *The New Marketing Manifesto* (London: Texere Publishing, 1999).

24 The driver for this trend may be a loss of confidence compounded by early 2000s losses in the stock market rather than a loss of brand power. *2001 Brand Loyalty Survey,* Carlson Marketing Company.

25 PIMS research as cited by Peter Burgess, "Customer Value Measurement for Competitive Advantage," *Admap,* no. 428 (May 2002).

26 Matthew Boyle, "Power Shift," *Fortune,* July 21, 2003.

27 Brian E. Kardon, "The New Rules of Branding," *The Advertiser* (October 1998).

28 Mark Kingsbury, "If Size Isn't Everything . . . What Else Matters?" (paper, Market Research Society Annual Conference, Brighton, JK, March 2002).

29 For a complete discussion, see Fournier, "Consumers and Their Brands."

30 See Stephen Pinker, *How the Mind Works* (New York: W. W. Norton, 1997), and Joseph LeDoux, *The Emotional Brain: The Mysterious Underpinnings of Human Life* (New York: Simon and Schuster, 1998).

31 For a complete discussion, see Gerald Zaltman, *How Customers Think* (Cambridge, Mass.: Harvard Business School Press, 2003), ch. 10. John Haugeland describes the speed of the unconscious, "[C]ompared to 'unconscious processing'. . . conscious thinking is conspicuously laborious and slow—not

a lot faster than talking." John Haugeland, *Having Thought: Essays in the Metaphysics of Mind* (Cambridge: Harvard University Press, 1998), 159.

32 Zaltman, *How Customers Think,* 10.

33 Harley-Davidson Web site, http://www.harleydavidson.com.

34 D. Court, "Uncovering the Value of Brands," *The McKinsey Quarterly* 4 (1996): 176–178.

35 Court, "Uncovering the Value of Brands."

36 G. Tellis, "Advertising Exposure, Loyalty and Brand Purchase: A Two-Stage Model of Choice," *Journal of Marketing Research* 25: 134–144.

37 Corporate Branding, LLC, http://www.corebrand.com.

38 Colin Lewis, "Murphy's Law Is Art of Measuring Brands," *Birmingham Post,* February 26, 2001, and "Brand New Day for Marketing Research," *Birmingham Post,* February 12, 2001.

39 Desmet et al., "The End of Voodoo Brand Management," *The McKinsey Quarterly* 2 (1998): 106–117.

40 Brand Finance, http://www.brandfinance.com.

41 Satmetrix Systems 2001 research. Referred to in Shaun Smith and John Wheeler, *Managing Customer Experience* (London: Prentice Hall, 2002): 27.

42 Melissa Berman, "The CEO Challenge: Top Marketplace and Management Issues, 2001," *The Conference Board* (January 2001), http://www.conference-board.org.

43 Frederick Reichheld, *The Loyalty Effect* (Cambridge, Mass.: Harvard Business School Press, 1996).

44 Research conducted by Eager Manager Advisory Services, July 2000. As reported in Tom Kellerhals, "Intellectual Capital," *Financial Service Marketing* 3, no. 5 (July 2001): 40.

45 Kirkland, the big Costco store brand, is steadily eating away at big Procter & Gamble brands. Wal-Mart's Ol'Roy dog food has surpasssed Nestle's Purina as the world's top-selling dog food. Boyle, "Power Shift."

46 As reported in T. Ambler, "Do Brands Benefit Consumers?" *International Journal of Advertising* 16, no. 3 (1997).

47 Ambler, "Do Brands Benefit Consumers?"

48 See http://www.brandchannel.com/features_effect.asp?id=195.

49 Mark Morford, "Lick Me, I'm a Macintosh: What the Hell Is Wrong with Apple That They Still Give a Damn about Design and Packaging and 'Feel'?" *SF Gate,* October 1, 2003. Original article found at http://www.sfgate.com/cgi-bin/article.cgi?file=/g/a/2003/10/01/notes100103.DTL.

50 The original Apple ad can be viewed at http://www.apple.com/hardware/ads/1984/.

51 Gerald Zaltman, "Lighting Up the Shadows" (presentation, Procter & Gamble's Future Forces Conference, Cincinnati, Ohio, September 1997).

52 For a complete discussion of brand communities, see Albert M. Muniz Jr. and Thomas C. O. Guinn, "Brand Community," *Journal of Consumer Research, Inc.* 27 (March 2001): 412–432.

53 Zaltman, "Lighting Up the Shadows," 197.

Chapter 2: Generic Customer Service Isn't Enough Anymore

1 As reported in the *London Sunday Times,* May 12, 2002.

2 For a complete discussion of the nostalgia factor and the role that brands play in evoking memories of the past, see Judith Langer, "What Consumers Wish Brand Managers Knew" (paper presented at Advertising Research Foundation Workshop, New York, April 1994).

3 For a complete discussion, see Fournier, "Consumers and Their Brands."

4 Nicholas Ind, "Living the Brand: Why Organizations Need Purpose and Values," *The Journal of the Marketing Society,* no. 15, (2001).

5 Ron Kaufman Web site, http://www.RonKaufman.com/bestof.html.

6 For a complete discussion of this topic, see Valerie S. Folkes and Vanessa M. Patrick, "The Positivity Effect in Perceptions of Services: Seen One, Seen Them All?" *Journal of Consumer Research, Inc.* 30 (June 2003).

7 Michael Edwardson et al., Consumer Emotions Study, SOCAP (Sidney, Australia, 2003): 2. Available through secretariat@socap.org.au.

8 Michael Edwardson's remarks to the annual SOCAP conference in Sydney, Australia, August 2003.

9 Jan Carlzon, *Moments of Truth* (New York: Ballinger Publishing, 1987).

10 Kevin Roberts, e-mail communication with the authors, January 2004.

11 See Folkes and Patrick, "The Positivity Effect in Perceptions of Services."

12 Nigel Cope, "Can Ratner Regain His Old Retail Sparkle?" *Independent,* July 28, 2003.

13 The PowerPoint presentation, while still available on some web sites, is no longer being circulated at the request of the author. He feels complete with Doubletree.

14 Michael Edwardson et al., Consumer Emotions Study, SOCAP (Australia, 2003): 2. Available through secretariat@socap.org.au.

15 David Haigh, "The Role of Brands and Brand Managers," *Brand Finance,* May 2000.

16 For a marketing perspective, see Michael D. Johnson, Eugene W. Anderson, and Claes Fornell, "Rational and Adaptive Performance Expectations in a Customer Satisfaction Framework," *Journal of Consumer Research* 21, no. 4 (March 1995): 695–707.

17 As quoted in H. James Harrington, "Creating Organizational Excellence— Part Five," *Quality Digest* 23, no. 5 (May 2003): 14, 54.

18 See Max Blackston, "Observations: Building Brand Equity by Managing the Brand's Relationships," *Journal of Advertising Research* (January 2000).

19 For example, see John Morrill, "How to Improve Profitability through Advertising," *Harvard Business Review* 4 (March–April 1970).

20 David Burrows and Juliet Williams, "Who Is Killing CRM?" *Admap* (July 2001).

21 These brand experts insist, "In order for the meaning of brands to become fully concrete, the mediated meaning derived from advertising and promotion must be negotiated with the lived experience of purchase and usage." Richard Elliot and Kritsadarat Wattanasuwan, "Brands as Symbolic Resources for the Construction of Identity," *International Journal of Advertising* 17, no. 2 (1998).

22 As reported in the *London Sunday Times*, May 12, 2002.

23 This specific model, typical of models used by brand strategists, is the work of Keith Syron, market research consultant, and is reprinted with his permission.

24 The Gallup Organization reports that 60 percent of CRM implementation has fallen significantly short of expectations. See William J. McEwen, "Is CRM All Hype?" *Gallup Management Journal* (April 22, 2202), http://gmj .gallup.com.

25 Sistrum Mystery Shopping research, http://www.hewson.co.uk.

26 "State of the Industry," American Society for Training and Development, 1998, http://www.astd.org/astd.

27 If you want to reminisce, you can hear the old "catch our smile" ad at http://www.catchoursmile.com/.

28 As reported at http://www.cactuswings.com/psa/.

29 E-mail communication from Linda Bloeth Bugbee with the authors reprinted with permission.

30 Statistic cited in Elizabeth Goodgold, "Talking Shop," *Entrepreneur* (September 2003): 65.

31 For a complete discussion about the history of branding in relationship to consumer culture, see Holt, "Why Do Brands Cause Trouble?"

32 There are dozens of books about Deming and the quality movement. Two such books are Mary Walton and W. Edwards Deming, *The Deming Man-*

agement Method (New York: Perigee Press, 1988), and W. Edwards Deming, *Out of the Crisis* (Boston: MIT Press, 2000).

33 As quoted by Rick Burns, "We Are Family: Making a Resort 'Our' Home," *Lodging HR* 3, no. 12 (March 2002): 1.

34 As quoted by Rick Burns, Ibid.

Chapter 3: Road Map to Branded Customer Service

1 A lack of understanding by managers about their own brands arises, in part, because of the confusion about the differences between branding and marketing. Marketing is part of an externally focused exercise where consumer preferences are analyzed and needs are assessed. Marketing also involves decisions about the best way to package products and services. Finally, marketing is the process of communicating products and services to the marketplace.

2 Prophet's 2002 *Best Practices Study,* http://www.prophet.com.

3 Ibid.

4 Valerie Folkes, professor at the Marshall School of Business, argues that because customers have "learned to treat information about each service provider as limited to that unique transaction," service firms will find "creating brand images challenging." Folkes and Patrick, "The Positivity Effect in Perceptions of Services."

5 The model of Wolff Olins, a UK branding company, suggests that brands manifest their central ideas through one of four means: product (e.g., automobiles); environment (e.g., luxury hotels or luxury shopping establishments); communication or competency (e.g., service organizations); or staff behavior (e.g., food services, public services). As cited in Leslie de Chernatony, Susan Segal-Horn, and S. Khan, "Characteristics of Successful Services Brands" (paper, Market Research Society Annual Conference, Brighton, UK, March 15–17, 2000).

6 The most recent statistics show Southwest carrying 9.8 percent of U.S. domestic traffic as of June 30, 2003. This is double its share from ten years ago. Southwest is now facing the challenge of competition from other low-cost carriers that are edging into its territory. Southwest is making changes that it describes as "tinkering with its model." Melanie Trottman, "Snack Attack: Slew of Competitors May Force Southwest to Shift Tactics," *Las Vegas Review-Journal,* December 26, 2003.

7 As quoted in Andy Milligan and Shaun Smith, eds., *Uncommon Practice* (London: FT Prentice Hall, 2002), 54.

8 Gwen Davis, "Chefs with Attitude," *Wall Street Journal Europe,* October 25-27, 2002, weekend edition.

9 Florence Fabricant, "New York Diners Toast a Modest Find," *International Herald Tribune,* October 22, 2003.

10 Bob Niedt, "Bear Facts," Retail Notebook, *Syracuse Post Standard,* October 4, 2002.

11 Statistics from Elizabeth Goodgold, "Talking Shop," *Entrepreneur* (September 2003).

Chapter 4: Defining Your Brand DNA

1 Clayton M. Christensen and Michael E. Raynor, *The Innovator's Solution* (Cambridge, Mass.: Harvard Business School Press, 2003), 15.

2 These were identified by Texas A&M University by Len Berry, Valerie A. Zeitham, and A. Parasuraman, "Quality Counts in Services Too," *Business Horizons* (May–June 1985): 44–52.

3 As interviewed by Steven E. Prokesh, "Competing on Customer Service: An Interview with British Airways Sir Colin Marshall," *Harvard Business Review* (November 1, 1995): 100.

4 See Nicholas Kochan, *The World's Greatest Brands* (London: Macmillan, 1996), and Christopher Lovelock et al., *Services Marketing* (London: Prentice Hall Europe, 1999).

5 For a complete discussion of the death of push marketing, see John Ingall, "Exploiting the Brand Experience," *Admap,* no. 426 (March 2002).

6 As quoted in Tyrell and Westall, "The New Service Ethos."

7 Seventeen out of twenty brands fail in their first two years of being introduced; those numbers are not that dissimilar from how many companies fail in their first two years. Susanna Hart and John Murphy, eds., *Brands— The New Wealth Creators* (New York: New York University Press, 1998).

8 This is particularly true today when ad agencies are aware that advertising does not have the pull it used to have. First, there are so many more places to advertise; no one placement gets as wide exposure as it used to, except perhaps events such as the Super Bowl, which is astronomically expensive for ad placement. Second, television watchers either mute or ignore their sets when a commercial comes on. Third, marketing experts now know that people like to "discover" their own brands, found through word of mouth. See "NBC Hopes Short Movies Will Keep Viewers from Flipping," *New York Times,* Business Section, August 4, 2003.

9 Mark Di Somma, in a confidential brand strategy paper.

10 Jesper Kunde, *Corporate Religion* (New York: Prentice Hall, 2000).

Chapter 5: Brand Power Tools:
Likability, Reinforcement, and Consistency

1 Humor seems to be the one absolute required to achieve likability. See the summary of *USA Today* and pollster Louis Harris and Associates of eleven thousand adults. Dottie Enrico, "Humorous Touch Resonates with Consumers," *USA Today,* May 13, 1996.

2 For example, rich media, broadband advertising about services and high-ticket products, seems to generate more likability. See "Rich Media Ads Score High on Banding and Recall, *Newsbytes News Network,* August 24, 1999.

3 Dennis Smith, "Do Ads Make Kids Want to Buy?" *Business Wire,* January 25, 1999.

4 Original research conducted in 1990 by Biel and Bridgewater seemed to indicate that customers were twice as likely to be persuaded to purchase by advertisements if they liked them than if they didn't. A. L. Biel and C. A. Bridgewater, "Attributes of Likable Television Commercials," *Journal of Advertising Research* 30, no. 3 (1990): 38–44. But more recent research from Massey University in New Zealand seems to suggest that when you actually measure to see whether people buy, likability is not necessarily the variable that influences purchase. See Janet Hoek et al., "Likability: A Behavioral Analysis," *ANZMAC* (2000), http://www.ANZMAC2000.com.

5 Tim Ambler points out that Mercedes is viewed by some consumers as being better than Lexus, simply because it has been making quality automobiles for a much longer time. Tim Ambler, "Do Brands Benefit Consumers?" *International Journal of Advertising* 16 (1997).

6 As quoted in Stuart Ewen, *All Consuming Images: The Politics of Style in Contemporary Culture* (New York: Basic Books, Inc., 1988).

7 The word *recognizable* is the one used by Bob Tyrell and Tim Westall to describe this phenomenon. They write, "Achieving a distinctive and easily recognizable personality in every aspect of the literal and metaphorical conversation the company has with its customers needs every part of the company to 'live the brand.' An economic and sustainable solution to this has yet to be fully developed." Tyrell and Westall, "The New Service Ethos."

8 For a complete listing of all the Virgin companies, visit the intensely branded Web page: http://www.virgin.com/uk/atoz/.

9 Richard Branson, foreword to Daryl Travis, *Emotional Branding* (Roseville, Calif.: Prima Venture, 2000).

Chapter 6: Culture Change:
The Bedrock of Brand Development

1 Collins, *Good to Great.*

2 Corporate Reputations Survey, *Fortune* 13, no. 4 (March 6, 1995): 54–60.

3 Tom Peters and Robert Waterman, *In Search of Excellence* (New York: Harper Collins, 1982).

4 Matthew Dearnaley, "'Unfair' Redundancy to Cost EDS $72,000," *New Zealand Herald,* January 12, 2004. Kotter and Heskett also cite the example of Time Inc., which in 1989 successfully blocked a hostile takeover bid by Paramount, arguing that its culture would be destroyed or changed by the takeover. John P. Kotter and James L. Heskett, *Corporate Culture and Performance* (New York: Free Press, 1992), 10.

5 Ashok Gopal, "Disengaged Employees Cost Singapore $4.9 Billion," *Gallup Management Journal,* October 9, 2003.

6 Lyle Spencer, "Improvement in Service Climate Drives Increase in Revenue" (paper presented at a meeting of the Consortium for Research on Emotional Intelligence in Organizations, Cambridge, Massachusetts, April 19, 2001).

7 Kotter and Heskett, *Corporate Culture and Performance.*

8 Ibid.

9 As cited in an interview with John Huey and Geoffrey Colvin. Jack Welch/ Herbert Kelleher Broadcast, *Fortune,* November 18, 1998.

10 Much has been written about emotional intelligence in recent years. We recommend the range of books by Daniel Goleman.

11 Private interview, August 2003.

12 Vodafone Staff Survey, April 2003. Percentages state the proportion of employees who "agreed" or "strongly agreed" with statements relating to these factors.

Chapter 7: Communicating to Ensure Brand Resonance

1 Thomas F. Gilbert, *Human Competence: Engineering Worthy Performance* (New York: McGraw-Hill, 1987), 90.

2 Ibid., 177–180.

3 John Case, *Open-Book Management: The Coming Business Revolution* (New York: HarperBusiness, 1995).

4 Robert Kaplan and David Norton, *The Balanced Scorecard* (Boston: Harvard Business School Press, 1996).

5 Kevin Thomson, *Emotional Capital* (Tulsa, Okla.: Capstone Publishing Ltd., 1998), 54.

6 Ibid.

7 Ibid., 85.

8 This sentence is based upon remarks by Felicity Stevens, an internal marketing specialist with whom TMI works.

9 Gilbert, *Human Competence,* 90.

10 Mark Di Somma, "Brand Attention Disorder," contribution to http://www.allaboutbranding.com, 2002.

11 Ibid.

Chapter 8: Internal Word of Mouth:
The Role of Brand Champions

1 Malcolm Gladwell, *The Tipping Point* (Boston: Little, Brown and Company, 2000).

2 Ed Keller and Jon Berry, *The Influentials* (New York, Free Press, 2003).

3 Gladwell, *The Tipping Point,* 132.

4 Ibid.

Chapter 9: Human Resources:
The Window to the Corporate Soul

1 For a good overview of the balanced scorecard concept, see Robert S. Kaplan and David P. Norton, "The Balanced Scorecard—Measures That Drive Performance," *Harvard Business Review* (January–February 1992): 71–79.

2 Mark Henderson, "Role Changes for Human Resources," *Sunday Star Times,* January 12, 1997.

3 Steven Greenhouse, "Help Wanted: But Only the Young, Hip and Blue-eyed Need Apply," reprinted in *International Herald Tribune,* July 12–13, 2003.

4 Ibid.

5 Shelly Branch, "Maybe Sex Doesn't Sell, A&F Is Discovering," *Wall Street Journal,* December 12, 2003.

6 See http://www.pretàmànger.com

7 Ibid.

8   The key players in the organization include Bernard Goldstein, whose vision it was to develop the gaming industry on the Gulf Coast and then eventually to expand his casino nationwide and now even internationally; Jack Gallaway, who was COO when TMI was first introduced to the Isle; Tim Hinkley, current COO; Robert Boone, vice president of human resourcs; and Cynthia Payne, director of cultural development, who keeps the vision alive across the many Isle properties.

9   Collins, *Good to Great,* 14.

10 Both of these programs have continued under the committed direction of Cynthia Payne, director of cultural development.

11 Statistics provided by the Isle of Capri. Average annual staff turnover rates in the casino industry's regional markets are 45 to 55 percent.

Chapter 10: Great Brands Are Supported from Within: The Role of Management

1   Michael T. Ewing et al., "Employment Branding in the Knowledge Economy," *International Journal of Advertising* 21 (2002). Ewing references M. C. Gilly and M. Wolfinbarger, "Advertising's Internal Audience," *Journal of Marketing* 62 (January 1998): 69–88.

2   Ind, "Living the Brand."

3   Rodd Zolkos, "Kemper Brand Image Stresses Core Values," *Business Insurance* 35 (July 16, 2001): 34.

4   Kemper Insurance Company, Kemper Annual Report (2001), 33.

5   James Heskett, "Lessons in the Service Sector," *Harvard Business Review* (March–April, 1987): 118–126.

6   "Hallmark Entertainment Network Launches Redesigned Brand Strategy," *Business Wire,* August 21, 2000.

7   For the fifth consecutive year, ASB Bank was rated New Zealand's number one major bank in terms of customer satisfaction in the highly respected University of Auckland survey of residential bank customers. It was also rated number one business bank for the third consecutive year in the university's business banking customer survey.

Chapter 11: Selling in a Branded World: Linking Your Brand Proposition to Your Sales Messages

1 The beginning of relationship marketing was explained by H. Hakansson and C. Ostberg, "Industrial Marketing: An Organisational Problem," *Industrial Marketing Management* (1975): 113–123. The idea was explained in relationship to services by L. L. Berry, *Relationship Marketing in Emerging Perspectives on Service Marketing* (Chicago: American Marketing Association, 1983), 25–28, and then applied to consumer sales by R. Oliver Christy and J. Penn, "Relationship Marketing in Consumer Markets," *Journal of Marketing Management* 12 (1996): 175–187.

2 See J. N. Sheth and A. Parvatiyan, "The Evolution of Relationship Marketing," *International Business Review* 4 (1995): 397–418.

3 Peter Drucker, in his customary precise and direct style, expressed it this way: "Marketing . . . is the whole business seen from the point of view of its final result, that is, from the customer's point of view. Concern and responsibility for marketing must, therefore, permeate all areas of the enterprise." Peter F. Drucker, *People and Performance* (New York: Harper & Row, 1977).

4 This idea has been expressed by numerous business leaders, including Andrew S. Grove (CEO, Intel Corporation), *One-on-One with Andy Grove* (New York: G. P. Putnam's Sons, 1987).

5 Adrian Payne, Martin Christopher, and D. Ballantyre, *Relationship Marketing for Competitive Advantage: Winning and Keeping Customers* (Oxford: Butterworth-Heinemann, Ltd., 1991).

6 Peter Jordan, "The High Tech Way to Hold the Anchovies," *VarBusiness* (January 1, 1996)

7 Panayiotis Kyzirdis et al., "Sales Management: Re-engineering the Sales Force for Relationship Marketing" (Symposium, European Society for Opinion and Marketing Research, Amsterdam, 1996).

8 Brand expert Daniel Finkelman reports that 20 percent of satisfaction in the industrial paper industry comes from the selling process, while 52 percent comes from customer service; in the automotive industry it is 16.8 percent from sales and 33.6 percent from customer service; and in telecommunications, less than 20 percent of satisfaction comes during the buying process, while 40 percent comes from customer service. Daniel P. Finkelman, "Crossing the Zone of Indifference," *Marketing Management* 2 (1993): 22–31.

9 Peter Jordan mentions this point in several of his articles. For example, see "How to Make the Computer Telephony Sales," *VarBusiness* (January 1, 1996).

10 Kyzirdis et al., "Sales Management."

11 As quoted in *Fast Company* (September 1988): 54.

Chapter 12: The Toolbox of On-Brand Exercises

1 Pete Wakeman at http://www.greatharvest.com.

2 J. I. Rodale, *The Synonym Finder* (New York: Warner Books, 1978).

3 Zaltman, *How Customers Think,* 32.

4 Zaltman cites a concrete example of this approach. "(A software company) trained help-line personnel to use movement and force metaphors during conversations with consumers ["Let's conquer the problem," "Let's get you going quickly," and "It's a slam dunk"]. The company also added the image of a lightning bolt near the help-line phone number on its packages and in its instructional materials. This image suggesting force and movement reassured potential purchasers that they could get fast, effective help when they needed it." Zaltman, *How Customers Think,* 95–96.

5 Zaltman, *How Customers Think,* 174.

6 "Grand Re-Brand," *Sean Callahan B to B* (April 24, 2000): 1.

7 B. Bachrach, "How to Influence Human Behavior," *Executive Excellence,* 12 (1995): 12–13.

Bibliography

Aaker, David A., and Erich Joachimshaler. *Brand Leadership*. New York: Free Press, 2000.

Asacker, Tom. *Sandbox Wisdom: Revolutionize Your Brand with the Genius of Childhood*. Manchester, N.H.: Eastside Publishing, 2000.

Bayler, Michael, and David Stoughton. *Promiscuous Customers: Invisible Brands; Delivering Value in Digital Markets*. Oxford, England: Capstone, 2002.

Beckwith, Harry. *Selling the Invisible: A Field Guide to Modern Marketing*. New York: Warner Books, 1997.

Bedbury, Scott, with Stephen Fenichell. *A New Brand World, 8 Principles for Achieving Brand Leadership in the 21st Century*. New York: Viking, 2002.

Clancy, Kevin J., and Peter C. Krieg. *Counter-Intuitive Marketing: Achieve Great Results Using Uncommon Sense*. New York: Free Press, 2000.

D'Alessandro, David F., with Michele Owens. *Brand Warfare: 10 Rules for Building the Killer Brand*. New York: McGraw Hill, 2001.

Davis, Scott M. *Brand Asset Management: Driving Profitable Growth through Your Brands*. San Francisco: Jossey-Bass, 2000.

Davis, Scott M., and Michael Dunn. *Building the Brand-Driven Business: Operationalize Your Brand to Drive Profitable Growth*. New York: John Wiley, 2002.

DeChernatony, Leslie. *From Brand Vision to Brand Evaluation*. London: Butterworth-Heinemann, 2001.

DeChernatony, Leslie, and Malcolm McDonald. *Creating Powerful Brands,* 3rd ed. London: Butterworth-Heinemann, 2003.

Dru, Jean-Marie. *Beyond Disruption: Changing the Rules in the Marketplace.* New York: John Wiley, An Adweek Book, 2002.

Dunmore, Michael. *Inside-Out Marketing: How to Create an Internal Marketing Strategy.* London: Kogan Page, 2002.

Gilmore, Fiona. *Warriors on the High Wire: The Balancing Act of Brand Leadership in the 21st Century.* London: Profile Books, 2003.

Gobe, Marc. *Citizen Brand: 10 Commandments for Transforming Brands in a Consumer Democracy.* New York: Allworth Press, 2002

Gobe, Marc. *Emotional Branding: The New Paradigm for Connecting Brands to People.* New York: Allworth Press, 2001.

Harvard Business Review on Brand Management. Cambridge, Mass.: Harvard Business School Press, 1999.

Ind, Nicholas, ed. *Beyond Branding.* London: Kogan Page, 2003.

Ind, Nicholas. *Living the Brand: How to Transform Every Member of Your Organization into a Brand Champion.* London: Kogan Page, 2001.

Kapferer, Jean-Noel. *(Re)inventing the Brand: Can Top Brands Survive the New Market Realities?* London: Kogan Page, 2001.

Kaplan, Robert S., and David P. Norton. *The Strategy-Focused Organization: How Balanced Scorecard Companies Thrive in the New Business Environment.* Cambridge, Mass.: Harvard Business School Press, 2001.

Kawasaki, Guy. *Selling the Dream: How to Promote Your Product, Company, or Ideas—and Make a Difference—Using Everyday Evangelism.* New York: Harper Business, 1991.

Knapp, Duane E. *The Brand Mindset.* New York: McGraw Hill, 2000.

Koehn, Nancy F. *Brand New: How Entrepreneurs Earned Consumers' Trust from Wedgwood to Dell.* Cambridge, Mass.: Harvard Business School Press, 2001.

LePla, F. Joseph, Susan V. Davis, and Lynn M. Parker. *Brand Driven: The Route to Integrated Branding through Great Leadership.* London: Kogan Page, 2003.

LePla, F. Joseph, and Lynn M. Parker. *Integrated Branding: Becoming Brand-Driven through Companywide Action.* London: Quorum Books, 1995.

Milligan, Andy, and Shaun Smith, eds. *Uncommon Practice: People Who Deliver a Great Brand Experience.* London: Pearson Education Limited, 2002.

Perry, Alycia, with David Wisnom. *Before the Brand: Creating the Unique DNA of an Enduring Brand Identity.* London: McGraw-Hill, 2003.

Pine, B. Joseph, and James H. Gilmore. *The Experience Economy: Work Is Theatre and Every Business a Stage.* Boston: Harvard Business School Press, 1999.

Pringle, Hamish, and William Gordon. *Brand Manners: How to Create the Self-Organisation to Live the Brand.* West Sussex, England: John Wiley, 1998.

Ries, Al, and Laura Ries. *The 11 Immutable Laws of Internet Branding.* New York: Harper Business, 2000.

Ries, Al, and Jack Trout. *Positioning the Battle for Your Mind: How to Be Seen and Heard in the Overcrowded Marketplace.* New York: McGraw Hill, 1986.

Ries, Al, and Jack Trout. *The 22 Immutable Laws of Marketing: Violate Them at Your Own Risk.* New York: Harper Business, 1994.

Rust, Roland T., Valarie A. Zeithaml, and Katherine N. Lemon. *Driving Customer Equity: How Customer Lifetime Value Is Reshaping Corporate Strategy.* New York: Free Press, 2000.

Schmitt, Bernd H. *Customer Experience Management: A Revolutionary Approach to Connecting with Your Customers.* New York: John Wiley & Sons, Inc., 2003.

Smith, Shaun, and Joe Wheeler. *Managing the Customer Experience: Turning Customers into Advocates.* London: Prentice Hall, 2002.

Temporal, Paul. *Branding in Asia: The Creation, Development and Management of Asian Brands for the Gobal Market.* Singapore: John Wiley, 2002.

Underhill, Paco. *Why We Buy: The Science of Shopping.* New York: Simon & Schuster, 1999.

Upshaw, Lynn B. *Building Brand Identity: A Strategy for Success in a Hostile Marketplace.* New York: John Wiley, 1995.

Wilson, Jerry R. *Word-of-Mouth Marketing.* New York: John Wiley, 1994.

Zyman, Sergio. *The End of Marketing as We Know It.* New York: Harper Business, 1999.

Index

About the Authors

Janelle Barlow, Ph.D., is president of TMI US, a partner with Time Manager International, a multinational training and consulting group. Janelle is coauthor with Claus Møller of the best-selling business book *A Complaint Is a Gift: Using Customer Feedback as a Strategic Tool,* published by Berrett-Koehler. She is also coauthor of *Emotional Value: Building Strong Relationships with Customers,* and *Smart Videoconferencing: New Habits for Virtual Meetings,* both published by Berrett-Koehler. Her book *The Stress Manager* is used in the popular TMI course by the same name. She also developed a management training program, Creativity Power: Unbind Your Mind, which uses 365 skill-building mental aerobic exercises called mind flexors.

Her doctorate was earned at the University of California at Berkeley, where she studied both political science and education. She has two master's degrees, one in international relations and another in psychology. She is a licensed marriage and family therapist. Janelle is married and has a son.

Twice awarded the prestigious International Trainer of the Year award by Time Manager International, Janelle works with and looks at brand images in exotic locations such as Croatia, India, Poland, China,

Peru, Portugal, Puerto Rico, and Papua New Guinea. She earned the designation of Certified Speaking Professional offered by the National Speakers Association, on whose national board Janelle is an elected member.

Prior to joining TMI, she was the founder of an educational corporation that produced major personal development rallies for thousands of people. While in her twenties, she lived in Taiwan for three years, where she developed a particularly keen sense of diverse ideas and approaches to management.

As a keynote speaker, consultant, and seminar leader, she draws upon her broad educational background and practical management experience. Over 100,000 people from all continents have participated in and been charmed by Janelle's training programs and speeches.

Paul Stewart is a director of TMI New Zealand, partner in the international consulting and training company Time Manager International. He studied economics and psychology at the University of Otago (New Zealand) and graduated with a bachelor of arts, first class honors. In his twenties he rose rapidly to the position of chief economist for the ANZ Banking Group (NZ), one of Australasia's leading banks, and became renowned as a leading business and economic commentator. In 1998, he was chairman of the Economics Committee of the New Zealand Bankers Association and was a member of the Government's Consumer Price Inflation review committee.

His growing passion for effective application of business strategy led him into the field of corporate strategy, brand development, and organizational effectiveness. Described as an outstanding leader at an individual, team, and company level, he has a rare ability to work with all levels of organizations, from boards and executives to operations teams and employees. As a senior executive, he managed complex corporate projects covering integrated brand development, merger communications, and cultural integration. During this time, he led teams that won awards for best corporate strategy and B2B Web sites and developed world-class brand strategies.

In 2002, he joined TMI New Zealand as a full-time executive and consultant and now works with a range of leading organizations on strategic initiatives around cultural transformation, integrated brand development, service delivery, emotional intelligence, and employee communications. He coaches and mentors emerging executives.

As a speaking professional and member of the National Speakers Association of New Zealand, Paul is a widely sought-after speaker on organizational development and business strategy. He was a founding board member of a regional economic development trust and is a trustee of a leading-edge think tank, the Future of People and Organizations. Paul is passionately committed to Leah, his partner in life and business, and their standard schnauzer named Max.

A Web site has been created for this specific subject at http://www.brandedservice.com. Janelle's telephone number in Las Vegas is 702-939-1800; her e-mail address is Janelle.Barlow@brandedservice.com. Paul's telephone number in Auckland is 64-9-373-4240; his e-mail address is Paul.Stewart@brandedservice.com. TMI US's Web site is http://www.tmius.com; TMI New Zealand's Web site is http://www.tmi.co.nz.

About Berrett-Koehler Publishers

Berrett-Koehler is an independent publisher dedicated to an ambitious mission: Creating a World that Works for All.

We believe that to truly create a better world, action is needed at all levels -- individual, organizational, and societal. At the individual level, our publications help people align their lives with their values and with their aspirations for a better world. At the organizational level, our publications promote progressive leadership and management practices, socially responsible approaches to business, and humane and effective organizations. At the societal level, our publications advance social and economic justice, shared prosperity, sustainability, and new solutions to national and global issues.

A major theme of our publications is "Opening Up New Space." They challenge conventional thinking, introduce new ideas, and foster positive change. Their common quest is changing the underlying beliefs, mindsets, institutions, and structures that keep generating the same cycles of problems, no matter who our leaders are or what improvement programs we adopt.

We strive to practice what we preach -- to operate our publishing company in line with the ideas in our books. At the core of our approach is stewardship, which we define as a deep sense of responsibility to administer the company for the benefit of all of our "stakeholder" groups: authors, customers, employees, investors, service providers, and the communities and environment around us.

We are grateful to the thousands of readers, authors, and other friends of the company who consider themselves to be part of the "BK Community." We hope that you, too, will join us in our mission.

Be Connected

Visit Our Website

Go to www.bkconnection.com to read exclusive previews and excerpts of new books, find detailed information on all Berrett-Koehler titles and authors, browse subject-area libraries of books, and get special discounts.

Subscribe to Our Free E-Newsletter

Be the first to hear about new publications, special discount offers, exclusive articles, news about bestsellers, and more! Get on the list for our free e-newsletter by going to www.bkconnection.com.

Participate in the Discussion

To see what others are saying about our books and post your own thoughts, check out our blogs at www.bkblogs.com.

Get Quantity Discounts

Berrett-Koehler books are available at quantity discounts for orders of ten or more copies. Please call us toll-free at (800) 929-2929 or email us at bkp.orders@aidcvt.com.

Host a Reading Group

For tips on how to form and carry on a book reading group in your workplace or community, see our website at www.bkconnection.com.

Join the BK Community

Thousands of readers of our books have become part of the "BK Community" by participating in events featuring our authors, reviewing draft manuscripts of forthcoming books, spreading the word about their favorite books, and supporting our publishing program in other ways. If you would like to join the BK Community, please contact us at bkcommunity@bkpub.com.